HOW I
LEARNED THE SECRETS
OF SUCCESS IN SELLING

Frank Bettger

ABOUT THIS BOOK

I F I WERE ASKED to name the one person who gave me the best advice I ever had in my life—it would unquestionably be a man who dedicated the greatest part of his life to helping others... *Dale Carnegie*, the man to whom I have dedicated this book. And here's why:

When I was a total and complete failure, it was in his personally conducted public speaking course—then in its first stages at the Y.M.C.A. in Philadelphia—that Dale Carnegie "introduced me" to *Benjamin Franklin's secret of success*... *the one big idea* which transformed my life from that of a down-and-out ex-ballplayer, twenty-nine years of age, unable to find a job of any kind, to a measure of success far beyond my wildest dreams!

Twelve years later, when I was in a position to retire, Dale asked me to help him extend his courses to most of the large eastern cities from Boston to Washington, D.C. Then, a few years afterwards, he induced me to join him on his lecture tours. We spent two consecutive years together conducting a series of one-week schools on "Leadership Training, Human Relations and Salesmanship" in most of the large cities throughout the U.S.

In Tulsa, Oklahoma, Dale began urging me to write a book—

this book. I said, "Dale, you know I only went to the sixth grade in grammar school. *I* couldn't write a book."

Dale said: "Listen, Frank, it is quite probable that you gave yourself a more *practical* education by forcing yourself to adopt Benjamin Franklin's *13 Weeks' Method of Success* than many men obtain by spending four years in college. You will be writing a *new* kind of book, the *first* ever published by a man who has acid-tested Franklin's idea. Your history has been so remarkable, Frank, this book will be helping and inspiring discouraged young men and women long after you are playing third base in Paradise!"

Since I had never written anything before in my life, Dale advised me to first write—as a warm-up—a book telling "how I raised myself from failure to success in selling." I followed his advice to the letter. In fact, I wrote two books on my experiences in selling.

Since then, Dale himself has gone on to join up with that team in Paradise . . . if he hasn't reached there yet, I know it's because he has stopped somewhere along the way to help somebody get ahead. He believed in, and practiced the Franklin philosophy: "The most acceptable service of God, is doing good to man."

I have Dale's picture, and Franklin's, on my desk before me as I write, urging me on. I am going to start this book the way life began for me . . . on a little back-street in one of the poorest sections of Philadelphia, Pa., at a time when it looked as though I had two strikes on me. . . .

Here it is. I hope you like it.

F. B.

TABLE OF CONTENTS

PART TWO

HOW I CHANGED MY LINE-UP

This book is dedicated to the memory of a man who dedicated his life to helping others — Dale Carnegie

Part One

"THE PRESIDENT WANTS TO SEE YOU!"

To the Reader

Old Bill Clark, famous baseball coach, used to yell to us from the coaching line when a game looked hopelessly lost: *"You can't most aways sometimes tell ... the least expected happens mostly."*

There was some kind of psychology in what he said and the way he said it, that made us believe something *was* going to happen—and it *frequently did!*

In PART I—the first nine chapters of this book—I think of them as the first *nine innings*— where "the least expected, happens mostly." Each inning I wanted to quit! Then, I'd remember something else Old Bill told us one day: "It's just when things seem at their worst that you musn't quit ...

Not until years later, did I realize that those disheartening nine "innings" were laying the groundwork, teaching me vital lessons, for a new and successful way of life! In fact, if it hadn't been for PART 1 of this book—PART 2 never could have been written; the two are inseparable. So, I am going to "lead off" with one of my baseball experiences in *the most fantastic ball-game ever played anywhere!* I hope you enjoy it.

Chapter 1

THE MOST FANTASTIC BALL GAME
EVER PLAYED ANYWHERE

As a PROFESSIONAL BASEBALL PLAYER, I played in almost every league from Montreal, Canada, to Galveston, Texas. But this fantastic game took place in Clifton Heights, Pennsylvania, in the little Delaware County League.

There were only four towns in this league: Chester, Upland, Clifton Heights, and Media. I was then playing third base for Media.

The rivalry among those four teams positively exceeded anything I ever witnessed in baseball! Well, let me give you a sample of what I mean.

At the end of the season, Media and Clifton Heights were tied for first place and playing the *final* game to decide the pennant. With two out in the ninth inning, we were ahead, 4-3. Clifton had the tying run on third base, but if we could get this next batter out, the game would be over and we'd be the *champions!*

This batter, a very fast runner, hit a sharp grounder between third and short. I was playing third base, and managed to

3

pick the ball up all right, but hurrying to get it away, threw wide of first base. When "Hads" Ogden, our big first baseman, stretched down the base line to grab the ball, the runner crashed head on into him and *down* they both went! Ogden looked up just in time to see the ball bouncing up the embankment—a natural "grandstand"—where hundreds of wildly excited Clifton Heights rooters were seated on the grass. Then an astonishing thing happened! *That ball bounded straight up a girl's dress!*

Up the hill dashed our first baseman. And around the bases dashed the runner. The other runner who'd been on third base had already scored the tying run.

The ground rules at Clifton Heights were: "*All you can get on an overthrow.*" But they had never seen a crowd like this at Clifton Heights. When Ogden reached the girl, he shouted "*Get up!*" but the pretty Clifton rooter just looked up at him in absolute defiance.

Ogden took a quick look around and saw the runner turn second and race like crazy for third. "Get up!" he shouted right in the girl's face. But you could see that she didn't intend to move a muscle.

Ogden took another fast glance at the runner, now rounding third base at an amazing burst of speed—with the winning run and the pennant. There wasn't a split second to waste. He grabbed the girl under both arms, yanked her to her feet and shook her violently. Down dropped the ball. Quick as a flash Ogden snatched the ball, threw it like a bullet straight into our catcher's hands. The catcher tagged the runner beyond any question of doubt.

"*Yer out!*" roared the umpire.

Leaping off the ground, the runner swung a left and right

uppercut landing flush on the unfortunate umpire's jaw, practically lifting him off his feet. Down he went! Runner on top of him! Instantly, the wildest free-for-all fight I have ever witnessed started all over the ball field! The few policemen were powerless. Five men, including the umpire, were removed to the Delaware County Hospital, and six to the County Jail.

That game taught me *never to underestimate the power of a woman.*

... Borton Weeks, prominent Delaware County attorney, president of the league, rendered a decision that night. He ordered the entire game to be replayed the following Saturday.

Now this was late in the summer, after the hunting season had opened. You may wonder why I mention this ... well, you'll be surprised!

No world series game was fought more desperately than this play-off game. The pitchers of both teams—in fact all the players—went into it as though their very lives depended on the outcome. The whole playing field had to be roped off all the way down to the woods. It looked as if everybody in Delaware County turned out to see this game, including the police. The crowd had split up, Media rooters on one side of the field; Clifton on the opposite side. Word got around that there was quite a lot of betting going on. Hundreds of people from Philadelphia had flocked out there to see the excitement. And I'm here to tell you they got it!

By a strange coincidence, when the game came down to the ninth inning, with two outs, the score stood exactly the same as the previous week: 4-3, favor of Media. But there was one important difference. Clifton had the bases full and their best batter up—in fact, he was the most dangerous hitter in the league. As he walked into the batter's box, murder was in his eyes.

Excitement? That crowd was delirious. "Drive the first pitched ball down into the woods!" pleaded the Clifton rooters.

Any kind of hit would score two runs and win the pennant for Clifton Heights! Everybody held his breath as our pitcher, Vernon Touchstone, wound up and threw that ball so fast none of the rooters saw it. But the batter saw it—and he wasn't waiting. He took a mighty Babe Ruth swing at the ball . . . and connected. But a groan went up from the Clifton crowd. To the utter dismay of all Clifton Heights, the ball went straight up in the air directly in front of home plate. All the runners were racing around the bases, but it was a thousand to one that our old reliable catcher, Joe Knotts, an ex-big leaguer, would catch the ball—and we would be the champions.

During this wild excitement, no one had noticed a couple of hunters come up out of the woods back of the roped-off crowd. They were wearing red hunters' caps and carrying guns. One of them was a Clifton Heights man and said to have had a pretty heavy bet on Clifton. At a glance, he saw the situation and raised his gun to his shoulder. Every living soul's eyes were on that ball. BANG! Twenty feet above our catcher's head, everybody saw the ball explode. It wobbled lopsided momentarily in mid-air, then disappeared back into the astonished crowd.

The week before I thought I'd seen everything, but that fight was only a "preliminary." Today was the windup! That gunshot touched off a fight to end all fights. Players of both teams and hundreds of crazy rooters swarmed all over the field as police and firemen attempted to break it up. Fists were flying everywhere. Some of the "strong boys" had devised a new system; they were working in threesomes: two of them would grab their victim, pin his arms behind him, while the third guy—with brass knuckles—took a hop, skip, and jump, planting a fast combination to the victim's jaw.

Before the police could break up the riot, the firemen had to turn their high-pressure hose on everybody. Both the Delaware County Hospital and the Fitzgerald Mercy Hospital were necessary this time—*and of course the county jail.*

. . . Reviewing these two games later, one sports writer wrote: "Unquestionably, these were the most fantastic ball games ever played anywhere. The wind-up fight never had its equal since Napoleon was defeated at Waterloo!"

Chapter 2

HOW I HAPPENED TO GET STARTED IN
PROFESSIONAL BASEBALL

I KNEW WHO THEY WERE the minute I saw them standing on our front steps ringing the doorbell. They were the two tough-looking bums I often saw lounging around the corners on Ridge Avenue, usually in front of McDaniel's Saloon. I was just arriving home from work wearing grimy, greasy overalls. I was now a plumber's helper.

"Are you Frank Bettger?" one of them asked.

"Yes," I answered, eyeing them suspiciously.

"We wantcha to play short-stop next Saturday mornin' fer McDaniel's Saloon against Donahue's Saloon," was the older one's surprising opening. "We're playin' the game up at Schutzen Park."

Both of them looked about "half-crocked."

"Why would I play for McDaniel's Saloon?" I asked. "I've never been in the place."

"Aw, that don't make no difference. Nobody pays no attention t' that," they both assured me.

"How did you happen to come ask *me* t' play?"

"Sparrow Sharp and Bowels McCarthy told us aboutcha. They saw youse play that riot game last fall out at Clifton Heights. Sparrow and Bowels are gonna play with us too. We'll pay youse five dollars!"

Two dollars a game was the most anybody had ever paid me to play ball before. The five dollars sounded good. But I knew the two guys they mentioned. They were "park sparrows," just bums in the park, would-be ballplayers who wouldn't work for a living. I had played out in Fairmount Park a couple of times with that gang. This "Sparrow" Sharp had the makin's of a big-leaguer if only he could let booze alone.

And I knew about those games at Schutzen Park. The main attraction was a keg of ice-cold beer on the players' bench—all you could drink for free. In addition, most of the players carried a flask on their hip. By the fifth inning everybody was staggering.

... "No," I thought to myself, "I can't play with those rummies. My mother could use the five dollars all right, but she would never consent to it. Mom violently hated booze. Whiskey had broken up our home. My father had died a drunkard's death, leaving her penniless with five small children, and the rent overdue on our little four-room, row-house. For years Mom had to take in washing and sewing besides going out to do a day's work, in order to feed and clothe us and keep us in school.

About this time, Carrie Nation, "The Kansas Cyclone," was in top form with her hatchet, smashing up saloons. Mom would have made a perfect running mate for Carrie.

So, I started to give these two bums an excuse about having something else to do on Saturday, when the older one broke in and said something that changed my mind completely. In fact, after I heard what he said, I believe I would have paid them to let me play.

"Listen, Kid," said he, "this'll give youse a chance t' bat against a big-league pitcher. 'Reds' Donahue is gonna pitch for his team!

That did it!

The following Saturday will always stand out in my memory, because it marked the end of my days as a plumber's helper.

McDaniel's Team made only six hits off "Reds" Donahue. But luck was with me, because I made four of them. We beat Donahue's 6-4. My hits brought in four of the six runs and I scored the other two myself.

I was surprised how seriously both teams took that game. Nobody got drunk that day—this game was for blood.

"Reds" Donahue had been Detroit's star pitcher for years. Of course, he had lost most of his speed, but he could still throw his famous wide-sweeping curve. And that's mostly what he kept pitching. McDaniel's bums put one foot in the water bucket and swung like an old rusty gate in a cold winter wind.

Back in the dressing room after the game, I could hear big Reds' powerful voice as he soaked himself under the shower. "Why you bums never woulda scored a run if it wasn't fer that kid. Who the hell is he anyhow? *Don't tell me he was ever in McDaniel's Saloon!*"

Word quicky got around the neighborhood about what "Kid" Bettger had done in that game. My pals down at the corner cigar-and-candy store said: "Now, Betch, here's your chance. 'Reds' Donahue can getcha a job playin' professional ball." Each night they pleaded with me to go see Donahue. But every time I thought about it, my stomach took a flip-flop. Once, I even got as far as the front door of Donahue's Saloon, then lost my nerve. Then one night some of the fellows tagged along with me. We heard "Reds' " booming voice coming out over the swinging doors. Suddenly, one of the gang gave me a monstrous shove—and there I was, right back of Donahue at the bar!

"Reds" glanced around to see what was the commotion. "What do *you* want here?" roared the ex-big-league pitcher, like he was reprimanding a twelve-year-old.

I managed to say: "Mr. Donahue, I'm Frank Bettger. I played that game against you up at Schutzen Park. I wondered if yuh could get me a job playin' ball?"

"Reds" straightened up and took a good look at me. "Are you that kid who played short-stop fer McDaniel's?"

"Yes, sir." I tried to smile.

"Why damn you!" he exploded, "I can getcha a job anytime yer ready tuh start out."

A few days later a telegram arrived at our house from Johnstown, Pennsylvania. It had my name spelled "B-e-t-c-h-e-r" (which is the way it sounds):

WIRE LOWEST TERMS AT ONCE TO PLAY WITH JOHNSTOWN IN THE TRI-STATE LEAGUE
                              CHARLES ATHERTON, MANAGER

If my mother had been home at the time to receive it, I never would have seen that telegram to this day.

That night, I was so scared I hardly ate my dinner. Later in the evening I went around to Donahue's. Most of the gang was with me. When "Reds" read the wire, he slammed me on the back and beamed all over. "Wire back tonight. Tell 'em yuh want $350 a month!" he roared.

The gang seemed as excited as I was as we walked down Ridge Avenue to the Western Union Telegraph office. Before we went in, I stopped. "Look, fellahs," I said, "I'm makin' eight dollars a week now. If Johnstown paid me $350 a month, I wouldn't be able to catch a ball."

The gang agreed with me, so we cut "Reds'" figure in half. I signed the wire Frank *Betcher*—the same as they had addressed me. And "Betcher" it stayed, as long as I was in baseball.

I didn't sleep much that night. The next morning I awoke with a fever of 103°. Mom quickly sent for the nearest doctor. Just before he arrived, a telegram was delivered. Mom opened it. It read:

TERMS ACCEPTED REPORT TO JOHNSTOWN AT ONCE

CHARLES ATHERTON, MANAGER

Upstairs she tore! I tried to explain, but she began to cry. Then the doctor arrived. He said it was just "grippe," but that I would have to stay in bed a few days. Mom pleaded with him to talk me out of becoming a ball player. "Doctor," she cried, "Frank has always had a bad heart. It would *kill* him!"

The doctor looked surprised. He had never seen me before. Out came his stethoscope again, and this time he examined me much more carefully.

"Who ever told you this boy has a bad heart?" he asked.

Mom told him about how I had been born with a weak heart, and that she never expected to raise me.

"Well," he assured her, "if your son ever had a bad heart, he sure has outgrown it. His heart is absolutely sound."

And to my great joy, he urged Mom to let me go to Johnstown. "It will be a *wonderful* thing for him!" he emphasized.

Doctor Thomas didn't know how right he was.

When I arrived in Johnstown, I expected them to play better ball than any team I had ever played with before, but I didn't imagine anything like what I ran into. The first team I played against—Williamsport—looked as good to me as some big league teams I had seen play in Philadelphia. In fact, Williamsport won the Tri-State League pennant that year, and seven of their players went to the big leagues. And their manager, Harry Wolverton, became manager of the Highlanders—later named the New York Yankees!

I couldn't have been more scared that first game if I had been caught in the Johnstown Flood. Charlie Atherton, the manager, seemed to understand and was like a father to me. Each day he did his best to build up my confidence.

Then came the first of the month. Pay Day! My first pay as a professional ballplayer! I practically ran to the post-office and mailed a letter home to my mother, special delivery, with a money order. It was one of the happiest moments of my life, as I wrote: "Mom, now you won't have to go out and do day work any more." I wept.

But the next day brought one of the biggest shocks of my life. Charlie Atherton was fired. Bert Conn, our centerfielder, became manager. And the first thing Conn did was *fire me*.

Bert Conn's eyes were cold as stone as he said:

"Frank, whatever you do after you leave here, for heaven's sake, wake yourself up and put some life and enthusiasm into your work!"

Ten days later I was "discovered" down in Chester, Pennsylvania by an ex-ballplayer named Danny Meehan. Danny only saw me play one game, but thought I belonged higher up. He said: "You're red hot, kid, you've got enthusiasm!" I laughed and told him I had just been fired because I *lacked* enthusiasm . . . and repeated to him Bert Conn's memorable "Farewell Address."

Within one week Danny induced New Haven, Connecticut to give me a trial. When I arrived in New Haven, it was one of those sweltering hot, midsummer days. My instructions were to report to the law office of C. J. Danahuer, prominent attorney in Connecticut, who was also president and principal owner of the New Haven Baseball Club. Danny had told me: *"The President Wants to See You!"*

I was amazed at the heavy traffic and bustling activity. I had never thought of New Haven as a Big City, only knew it was the town where Yale University was located. I found the office all right, and as I entered the large reception room, it looked deserted for the week-end.

Just then a boy came out of a private office. When I told him who I was, he turned back quickly without a word and nearly burst out laughing. I heard him say, "Mr. Danahuer, Betcher is here!"

Out rushed Mr. Danahuer. When he saw me, he stopped short, gulped, then turned sharply to the boy and exploded: *"WHERE is Betcher?"*

The boy looked as scared as I was. Pointing to me, he said, *"There he is, sir."*

The big man stepped over closer. He just couldn't believe what he was seeing. "Are *you* Betcher?" he asked in dismay.

All I could do was just nod.

I knew I didn't look right, but I didn't realize that my appearance was so ridiculous. I was two months overdue for a haircut, so I kept my straw hat on to hold down my hair. The style of that hat had never before been seen in New England--the rim wasn't a half inch wide! I had grown pretty thin that summer, my face was drawn and my trousers hiked a couple of inches above the white tennis shoes I wore. On the train that morning, I began squeezing a boil right on the end of my turned-up nose. I finally brought the boil to a head, but now it was swollen to twice its size, a frightening thing to behold! Standing there, holding a small pasteboard suitcase, I guess I wasn't the promising looking ballplayer Mr. Danahuer had pictured. . . .

If poor old Danny Meehan had walked in there that minute, he might have been murdered. In a deep, thunderous voice, Mr. Danahuer said, "Why, these are MEN playing up here in this league!"

He walked over to the window and stared out for a while. He was wearing an expensive-looking dark business suit. With his back still turned to me, he said: "Meehan recommended you so highly, we let Fitzgerald, our second-baseman, go to the Giants last night."

There was a quiet spell. Suddenly, Mr. Danahuer walked back into his office and slammed the door. He was gone about five minutes. It seemed like an hour.

"What a fool I was to leave Chester," I thought. "Why should I think I could make good in a league that's in the same class with Johnstown. . . ."

Then Mr. Danahuer came out again. To my surprise he asked, "Could you eat a little lunch, son?" He really looked sorry for me.

We went down to a small lunchroom in the basement of the building. Sitting on stools at the counter, we each had a sandwich and coffee. There was complete silence. I sensed his taking several glances straight at that boil on the end of my nose. By this time, it was aching like no boil I'd ever had before! Pretty soon he asked, "How old are you?" I said, "Eighteen." Looking doubtful, he said, "You don't look it."

Later, I heard him say, "I don't know what we'll do today. We've got nobody who can play second base." He seemed to be talking to himself.

I said, "Can't you give me a chance . . . just today?" My eyes filled up as I spoke.

I've always believed if I hadn't asked for the chance, he would have sent me back without a trial.

He took me out to the ballpark, located at Savin Rock. I soon found myself sitting on a stool in the far corner of the locker room. The President was talking to Jerry Connell, captain of the team. Jerry was the powerfully built "Rocky Marciano" type. He took a couple of fast glances at me and looked disgusted. Later, he came over and without a word chucked a uniform in my lap. It was Fitzgerald's!

Most of the players were already out on the field, and I could hear a noisy Saturday crowd in the stands. As I put on that uniform, I began to get the same frightening, nervous tension I'd had in Johnstown. Then I thought I heard Bert Conn's voice, just as clearly as if he were sitting alongside of me: ". . . *wake yourself up and put some life and enthusiasm into your work!*" And then Danny Meehan's voice too, saying: "*You're red hot, Kid—you've got it!*"

Bert Conn's words, and Danny's, seemed to crowd out every other thought. Although the temperature was a hundred degrees in the shade, I ran around the field like a man electrified. I whipped the ball around to the other infielders like it was shot out of a rifle. It was a close and exciting game. With the score tied at 3-3 in the eighth inning and two out, I made a base hit to left field, rounded first base like mad—right on to second and slid into the bag with such force and excitement that the ball got away from the second baseman. I kept going like crazy, the same thing happened at third, and at home—and so I got a home run on a single!

The players said I acted like a "demon on the loose!"

Mr. Danahuer came down to the front of the grandstand, leaned out over the railing and violently shook my hand, shouting in my ear: "You're O.K., kid! Keep going! The crowd *loves* you!"

That turned out to be the winning run of the ballgame. The next day, the New Haven papers said there had never been such a human dynamo! They began calling me "Pep" Betcher, the Life of the Team! I mailed those clippings back to you-know-who in Johnstown! Can you imagine the expression on Bert Conn's face, as he read about "PEP" Betcher—the dub he'd tied a can to only three weeks before—*for being lazy!*

I wasn't lazy—I was scared. It was fear that was holding me back. But when I began to force myself to act enthusiastic, my nervousness began to work *for* me. My fear became enthusiasm—literally, "A Demon on the Loose!"

I also mailed a set of clippings to Danny Meehan, with a letter telling him how I had heard his voice that day in the locker room just before the game ... but he never got my letter. Poor Danny had gone on to his reward that very day; in fact I learned later—the very *hour* that I was out on the field making the winning play for New Haven.

Chapter 3

HOW THIS IDEA RAISED MY BATTING AVERAGE
FROM .238 TO OVER .300
AND PUT ME IN THE BIG LEAGUES

Soon AFTER THE SEASON CLOSED in New Haven, a lot of publicity started about a third major league being organized—"The Union League." Sam Kennedy, New Haven's star first baseman when I played up there, was appointed manager of Baltimore. Sam came to see me in Philadelphia. He showed me a list of many National and American League players who had signed up in the new league. He made me an offer too good to turn down. Sam said: "Frank, this makes you a *big leaguer!*"

So, I signed with Baltimore.

Well, this was the rainiest season ever known in baseball. One stretch of ten days, it poured rain continuously. High salaried ballplayers were sitting around the hotel lobbies and eating three big meals a day. When we did get out to play, the weather was so cold and threatening, only small crowds turned out. So the Union League went broke. After playing a double-header on the Fourth of July, the new big league threw in the sponge and disbanded.

All the players who had "jumped" from organized baseball, were blacklisted for one year. Therefore, I played the balance of the season with Hazleton, Pennsylvania, in the "outlaw" Atlantic League. The following year, when I was reinstated, I was awarded to Greenville, South Carolina, at the time the lowest class league in organized baseball.

But this turned out to be a blessing in disguise! I loved Greenville. And the people treated me like a king even though I couldn't get started hitting. One day, Tommy Stouch, our manager, said: "Frank, if you could hit, the big leagues would be after you."

I said: "Is there anyway I could learn to hit?"

"Put that *enthusiasm* of yours into it and you'll learn to hit," declared Tommy.

I thought he was joking. I said, "How could I put *enthusiasm* into hitting?"

"Your whole trouble is poor timing," declared Tommy. "You can perfect your timing if you will go out to the ballpark every morning and hit three hundred balls. That will take *enthusiasm*, won't it?"

It never would have occurred to me how to put enthusiasm into hitting. But now, I got so excited over the idea that I tried to get a few of the other players on the team to try it with me.

They told me I was crazy. They said a northerner just couldn't stand the hot southern sun both morning and afternoon. But my roommate, Ivy "Reds" Wingo, a brick top freckled-faced young catcher from Waycross, Georgia, said he would like to try it with me. We found some boys who were glad to earn a few nickels and we went out early every morning before the sun got too hot. "Reds" and I each hit three hundred balls, and had a lot of fun doing it.

At the time "Reds" and I started this secret practice, my batting average was .238—averaging 5 hits out of 21 times at bat. The difference was only one additional hit each twenty times up, but at the end of the season that little difference raised my batting average to .300, gave me more hits than any other player in the Carolina League—and I woke up one morning to find myself on a train bound for New York City . . . to join the *St. Louis Cardinals!*

Within one hour after I arrived in New York to join the Cardinals—at the famous Polo Grounds—an astounding thing happened—a *"Believe It or Not" event never before nor since recorded in Major League history!*

I met the manager, Roger Bresnahan, in the locker room and he introduced me to a couple of the other players. Most of the players were already out on the field practicing, so, when I got out there they didn't even know who I was. But when the game started, there I was sitting on the bench in a St. Louis Cardinal uniform rubbing elbows with those great players I'd been reading about for years. It was like a dream come true. I was floating on air.

The biggest crowd I had ever seen was packed in the stands, and a perfect baseball day. I wasn't a bit nervous, wasn't going to play (that's what I thought). All I had to do was sit there and enjoy the game. *And I was being paid for this!* Christy Mathewson was pitching for the Giants . . . the immortal Christy Mathewson, master of the famed *fade-away pitch*, probably the greatest pitcher in baseball. "Big Chief" Meyers, the Indian, was catching. "Hank" O'Day, famous umpire, was behind the plate calling balls and strikes. And there was John "Muggsie" McGraw, famous manager of the Giants, pacing back and forth in front of the Giants bench. They all looked exactly like the pictures I'd seen of them for years.

Miller Huggins, captain and second baseman of the Cardinals, was up at the bat. Huggins didn't know it, but just before the game started, Mathewson had a talk with Hank O'Day, the umpire. Matty showed Hank a clipping he'd cut out of the newspaper that morning—a picture of Huggins, and an article about his having scored more runs than any other player in the big leagues so far that season.

"Now, Hank," explained Matty, "I'll tell you *why* Huggins scored more runs . . . he's on base more than anybody else . . . he's on base more, because he gets more bases on balls! To start with, he's only five foot six inches tall, then he stands in a low crouch over the plate. When the ball comes in, he takes that long stride and ducks . . . and you've got to get that ball through a derby hat to be called a strike. Hank, all I ask you to do today is call a strike on Huggins as you do when he is standing up in the position he does when he *intends* to hit the ball!"

Well, Huggins didn't know about this, so there he was in that low crouch over the plate. Mathewson wound up and delivered the ball with terrific speed right over the heart of the plate. But by the time Huggins took his long stride and ducked, there was the ball a foot over his head!

"S T R I K E O N E !" yelled Hank O'Day.

"What for?" snarled Huggins, as he leaped back and pushed his face under the Umpire's nose.

There was only one big thing about Huggins: he had the biggest mouth for a little guy I ever saw. Positively from where I sat on the bench, it looked as if his head was on a hinge at the back of his neck, and every time that big mouth opened his whole head seemed to move up and down on the hinge.

Hank O'Day never even blinked an eye. Finally, in disgust, Huggins walked back into the batter's box, pounded his bat violently on the plate, and again took that low crouch.

Mathewson had marvelous control. Again he delivered a terrific fast one in exactly the same spot. Again Huggins took that long stride and ducked, the ball passing a foot over his head.

"S T - R I K E T W O ! !" roared Hank O'Day.

"*What for?*" screamed Huggins, whirling around and leaping at the Ump like a rattlesnake. His big mouth opened up and down breathing fire into O'Day's face.

Up came the Umpire's hand pointing toward the Cardinals' bench: "*Out of the game for you!*"

Huggins raised his bat as though he was going to bounce it off the umpire's head. But all Hank did was slowly move his arm around in the direction of the clubhouse. Now Huggins began moving fast, back to the bench. Because if the umpire's finger got around to pointing at the clubhouse, Huggins would have to leave the grounds, automatically suspended for ten days, *without pay.*

Up to this point, I was having the greatest thrill of my life. *But there was a sudden change of events!* Bresnahan leaned forward, looking down among all the other players on the bench. I was sitting at the far end and his eyes just happened to catch my eyes. "Betcher," he yelled, "get a bat and go up and hit for Huggins!"

"Me?" I asked in dismay. Bresnahan nodded yes.

Well, you've heard me say I must have been born with two strikes on me. That's how I broke into the big leagues. And *Christy Mathewson* pitching!

Now I had brought a bat up from Greenville that I thought was the greatest bat I'd ever had in my hands. But do you suppose, in my excitement, I could find that bat? Why the Cardinals had more bats lined up in front of their bench than we had in the entire Carolina league! In embarrassment,

I picked up any bat and started for the plate. "Holy smokes," I thought to myself, "this is the heaviest bat I ever had in my hands." Then, as I walked, I noticed that my knees were trembling, and I began to feel weak all over. I felt as though I was walking up a steep hill and wasn't sure whether I was going to make it.

In those days there were no loudspeakers. The umpires were the loud speakers! Hank O'Day had never seen me before, so as I approached the plate he stepped over to me and asked: "Yer name?"

I was so scared I couldn't speak.

"*Yer name!*" repeated Hank right in my face.

By this time I couldn't even swallow.

I'll never forget the look of contempt on Hank's face as he turned his back on me, took off his cap, looked up at the press-box and in a tremendous voice yelled:

"AH–WAH . . . batting for Huggins!"

Now I noticed that these big leaguers always knocked the mud off the cleats of their shoes with their bat. Well–I hadn't been anywhere to get mud on the cleats of my shoes, but I wanted to look like a big leaguer, so I stepped into the batter's box and began very nonchalantly tapping the soles of my shoes with my bat. But I overlooked one very important technique: these big leaguers never do that while they are *in* the batter's box!

So, while I was looking down, tapping the soles of my shoes, Mathewson pitched. Just as I looked up, there was the ball coming straight at my head. I ducked, but the ball took that famous fade-away curve right down over the heart of the plate.

"S T R I K E   T H R E E . . . YER OUT!" roared Hank O'Day.

And for the first and *only* time in the history of baseball, a

3

player broke into the big leagues by striking out on one pitched ball!

On my way back to the Cardinal's bench, I heard McGraw yell, "Don't sign 'til you hear from me!"

The players on the bench were in convulsions; a couple of them were rolling on the grass. Bresnahan was standing along-side the water cooler, one foot up on the top step of the dugout, holding a full glass of water in his hand. With a straight face he said: "Betcher, here's your drink of water. I had it poured out for you even before you got up there!"

That night in the hotel, the players gave me such a terrific ribbing, I wished I hadn't gone into the dining-room. But after dinner, a surprising thing happened. Miller Huggins pulled me aside in the lobby: "Who are you rooming with, Betch?" he asked. I told him I didn't know; I hadn't been given a room yet. He said, "How would you like to bunk with me?" I said, "Sounds great!" Hug walked over to the desk clerk, and in a few minutes came back, handed me a key and said, "Get your suitcase and take it up."

Later, Huggins told me he'd had a roommate who talked too much. That told me what he expected from me—and I gave it to him. I thought to myself: "I want to find out how he *thinks*."

I found out. *He thought things through!* Huggins was the silent type. An educated man, a college graduate, actually had practiced law in Cincinnati, his home town. He was the shrewd-est and smartest baseball man I've ever known. I was anxious to learn, and he never seemed to tire of my asking questions—probably because he found me to be one of the world's best listeners.

So, what I thought was the toughest break a greenhorn rookie ever had happen to him, turned out to be lucky after all. In fact, it proved to be one of the luckiest breaks I ever had in my life! You will understand why when I come to it a little later on.

Chapter 4

I HAD TO GET WINGO BACK

You MAY BE WONDERING what happened to my Greenville roommate, Ivy "Reds" Wingo. "Reds" was only eighteen years old, had brilliant brick-red hair, a million freckles, a contagious laugh--and a highly exaggerated idea of my ability as a ballplayer.

I often wished I was half as good as "Reds" thought I was. He followed me around everywhere I went while I was in Greenville, as if I were some sort of hero. I enjoyed this for a while, it was very flattering. But finally, I became annoyed and found myself trying to avoid him.

However, soon after I left Greenville and got up to St. Louis, I missed Wingo something awful. I discovered that "Reds," unknowingly, had meant more to my baseball career than I realized. His amazing confidence in my ability made me feel like I was twice the man I was. For example, in a close game, if I came to bat at a critical time with runners on the bases, Wingo's wild excitement showed me that he just knew I'd come through with a hit. I couldn't let him down.

But now—in St. Louis—I was only another bench-warming rookie. And I couldn't hit from the bench . . . my bat wasn't long enough. My only claim to distinction as a big leaguer was that I was able to strike out on one pitched ball.

I thought: If I had "Reds" Wingo here with me, he'd tell these big leaguers how good I am. *I had to have "Reds" back!*

Then one day there was a bad accident. Jack Bliss, the Cardinals' third-string catcher, broke his leg. That put him out for the balance of the season. So the Cardinals purchased a catcher named Kelly from Milwaukee. I watched Kelly in action for several days. To me, he looked like "slow motion" compared with Wingo.

Here was my chance to get "Reds" back.

I began to tell Bresnahan about Wingo. I said: "Roger, he's very young, but he is going to be one of the greatest catchers in baseball. He's got the most wonderful throwing arm of any catcher I ever saw!"

"Is he a better catcher than Kelly?" asked Bresnahan.

"I don't know," I answered, "I never saw Kelly catch." (They were only using Kelly to catch during batting practice and to warm up pitchers.)

Well, the more I saw of Kelly, the more certain I felt that he wasn't in Wingo's class. Every chance I got, I would tell Bresnahan more about my Greenville roommate. Each time, this smart manager would ask me the same question: "Is he a better catcher than Kelly?"

My answer was always the same: "I don't know. I never saw Kelly catch in a game."

All this time, I'm just warming the bench and getting nothing but hemorrhoids. I was desperate. There wasn't anything I wouldn't do if I thought it would get my "confidence-builder" back again.

One day I said: "This boy Wingo can *hit*. He bats left-handed, and he can really belt that ball!"

Now, Roger asked a different question: "How is he on foul balls?"

"Terrific!" I declared. "He wears tennis shoes when he catches."

"Why?" asked Roger, surprised.

"In Greenville," I explained, "the roof of the grandstand only covers the back half of the stand. To protect the crowd from foul balls, there's a heavy wire screen stretching from the low rail in front of the stand up to the roof. The screen has sagged a bit, forming a belly in the midde. The instant a batter fouls the ball back, Wingo jerks off his mask, races to the grandstand, leaps onto the screen and runs up directly over everybody's head and catches the ball as the crowd stands up and cheers like mad."

THAT DID IT!

Only a few days later, a foul tip right off the bat fractured Bresnahan's thumb on his right hand. The doctor said he would be out of the game two or three weeks. The next day, Bresnahan disappeared. Somebody said Roger had gone off on a "scouting trip."

Ten days afterward, we were playing in Cincinnati. During the game I saw Roger come from under the stand and sit on our bench. "The Duke" was wearing a handsome new sports suit. His hand was still bandaged.

I was playing third base that day. As I came in after the inning ended I was surprised when he stepped out to meet me with the most friendly smile he had ever given me. "Well, I signed up Wingo," he said.

"*Do you mean Wingo is coming with us?*" I practically shouted.

"That's right," grinned Roger.

"What do you think of him?" I asked, all excited.

"Best damned lookin' young catcher I ever saw," declared Bresnahan. "But listen, you son of a z*z*z!, I stayed in Greenville a whole week *and I never saw him run up that screen once!*"

Chapter 5

"THE PRESIDENT WANTS TO SEE YOU!"

I HAVE A CLIPPING in my scrapbook that tells about my throwing a ball 356 feet nine inches—within fourteen yards of the world's record. At the time, it was said to be the second longest throw in baseball. Then, suddenly, two years after joining the Cardinals, while playing in Chicago one day, Frank Schulte, slugging outfielder of the Cubs, hit a swinging bunt down the third base line. I ran in, full speed, picked up the ball and attempted to throw it to first base—in the opposite direction. Something snapped in my shoulder. I called over to Huggins at second base: "Tell 'em not to hit any more down here, Hug." He yelled back, "Why?" *Something happened to my arm on that last throw*, I signalled.

Huggins went right in to Bresnahan and said, "We'd better get somebody else down there at third base. Frank's hurt himself."

At the time it wasn't thought to be serious, but that night I couldn't lift my arm to eat.

Nothing kills the spirit of a ballpayer like a bad arm. The following season, when my arm failed to come around, St. Louis put me on sale in baseball's bargain basement—the "waiver route." But no other National League team bid for me. So the Cardinals loaned me to Montreal, Canada, in the International League.

When I bid Huggins goodbye, he said, "Frank, this is a lousy business for a fellow with a glass arm. Why don't you get into something else while you're young enough to learn?"

. . . In Montreal, I played right field. When a ball came out there the second baseman raced out to me to relay the ball back to the infield. I had to snap the ball to him underhand!

Several weeks later the manager, "Kitty" Bransfield, came to me and said, "Frank, *the President wants to see you!*"

The president's name was Litchenstein. He was the owner of a number of ships on the St. Lawrence, conducting a prosperous commerce up and down the river. As I entered his office on the waterfront, he was pacing back and forth, head down, hands clasped behind him, dictating letters to his secretary. He was a very short man, and looked more like Napoleon than Napoleon looked like himself.

I remained standing quietly. Pretty soon he looked up and said: "Frank, we don't believe your arm will ever get better in this cool climate. There are too many windy days. We think if you get down South, the warm climate might bake out your arm and you'll have a chance. Last night I called St. Louis and talked with Bresnahan. They've decided to send you to Chattanooga, Tennessee, in the Southern League."

As his secretary handed me an envelope, Mr. Litchenstein explained: "That's your ticket and pullman. Your check is in there paying you up to date. . . ."

All night on the train I tossed in my berth, wide awake. There I was—*a young man on his way down* . . . .

When I arrived at the St. Charles Hotel in New Orleans, where Chattanooga was playing for a few days, I met the manager, "Kid" Elberfield, a former big-leaguer. First thing he asked was: "What's wrong with you, Frank?"

"I hurt my arm, Kid," I told him frankly, "but I believe it's gonna be all right again soon."

It was plenty hot in New Orleans and I was encouraged how much it helped my arm. However, five days later, when we arrived in Chattanooga, the "Kid" said to me . . . *"The President wants to see you!"*

I said, "Now?"

"Yes, right now," nodded Elberfield—and I didn't like the way he said it.

This president's name was Patton. He was a wealthy man, owned the ball-club, owned the Patton Hotel, and a chain of other hotels throughout the South.

When I arrived at his office in the Patton Hotel, an attractive girl stepped out, said Mr. Patton was tied up in a meeting and would be unable to see me. She handed me an envelope, unsealed. I removed the typewritten letter. It read:

> This is to notify you of your unconditional release by the St. Louis National League Baseball Club and the Chattanooga Baseball Club, effective immediately. Enclosed find check covering salary to date, and an additional ten days in accordance with your contract.

I couldn't have been more stunned if somebody had hit me on the head with a baseball bat. Reeling out through the lobby of the hotel, I was so dazed I didn't know where I was walking. Later, I found myself out on a high bridge over the Tennessee River. A little mongrel dog was following me. I never had any human being look at me with more sympathy.

I leaned against the rail of the bridge and wept. Nobody was in sight, so I just let go. I felt beaten and crushed. Everything seemed hopeless to me now. As I looked into the river, tears streamed down my cheeks and dropped into the water far below. There is no greater disappointment in life than when a man is disappointed in himself. If I had any idea of suicide, there would have been a perfect place to jump.

I believe the little dog sensed that I might be thinking of jumping because he stood on his hind legs, put his front paws up on me as high as he could reach, and let out a pitiful little cry. His wailing sounded like he was pleading with all his heart for me *not to jump*. His eyes looked right into my eyes, trying to comfort me.

Nobody could have consoled me and given me more comfort that morning than that little mongrel. In fact, I was in such distress, I didn't want to see a living soul. But I could cry as hard and as much as I wanted with the poor little fellow, and he seemed to understand.

Do you know, I don't believe a pure-bred dog could have given me the sympathetic understanding that this dog did. He probably had a few tin cans tied to him in his time, just as I had, and he understood exactly how I felt that morning . . . *nobody wanted me.*

Later, when I walked off the bridge and patted my wonderful little friend on the head and thanked him for helping me to face my failures, he looked so happy and wagged his tail knowingly; then watched me walk up the street. When I turned the corner I looked back, and sure enough he was still watching me, and seemed to be urging me on.

When I arrived back at the little old hotel where I had slept the night before, I meet *"Gabby" Street*, our catcher, who a few years afterward became manager of the St. Louis Cardinals. Gabby noticed something was wrong. "What's the matter, Betch?" he asked.

I couldn't talk. I just handed him the letter. He read it,

looked at me in amazement and said: "*Why you looked like
the best damned ballplayer in the league to me!*"

I'll never forget "Gabby." He gave me more than sympathy.
He walked me around to a telegraph office and, at his own
expense, wired several of his friends, managers of teams in
various parts of the country. Only *one* of them replied, Galveston, in the Texas League.

Two days later I was in Galveston. My arm had improved
so much in the hot southern sun that they put me on third
base, my favorite position. I hit well for Galveston; timely
hits, driving in runs. Then, suddenly, one day I threw the ball
and I thought my arm had come off! *I knew I was through.*

A couple of days passed. The manager came to me. I knew
by the expression on his face what he was going to say, so I
said it with him:

"*Frank, the President wants to see you!*"

It got so that every time a president wanted to see me I
knew what it meant. This was the fourth president who wanted
to see me that season, and they all had the same technique.

By now, I had four cans tied to me in four leagues!

One of Galveston's players said, "Frank, you've made a new
all-time record for yourself in baseball. You've hit the all-time
low, going from the Big Leagues to Class AA, Class A, Class
B—all in one season."

I thought I might just as well go all the way down those
back steps, so I wired Charlotte, North Carolina, a city I always
loved. I had been somewhat of a favorite there when I was
sold from the Carolina League to St. Louis. They wired back:

. . . COME TO CHARLOTTE AT ONCE . . . FANS ALL
EXCITED . . .

I was met at the railroad station in Charlotte by another
president—George Wearn, principal owner of the team. Mr.

Wearn was a lumber man and he didn't have any cans with him. Instead, he had a lot of red hot baseball fans with him. And they gave me a reception that night like I was Ty Cobb or Babe Ruth!

I told them I was in good condition—all except my arm. That I couldn't break a pane of glass. "That's all right," declared the manager. "We'll play you on first base where you won't have to throw."

Charlotte had the biggest crowd out to see the game the next day that they'd had all season. My first time at bat, everybody stood up and cheered. And was I lucky! The first ball pitched, I hit against the left field fence for a double! The crowd yelled like I'd just won the pennant for Charlotte!

For three days every ball I hit happened to go safe.

The fourth day we went to Raleigh, the capital city of North Carolina. It was a dark, cloudy day. First time at bat I swung . . . the ball shot in . . . hit me just about the wrist . . . and broke my arm. *I was through with baseball.* I had set a record by tumbling all the way down the back steps of baseball in one season—from the Major Leagues to Class "D," the lowest class in organized baseball.

The only man I ever heard of who played in more leagues, and slept in more beds in one year than I did, and is sometimes popularly referred to as the Father of his Country, was George Washington.

But I'd had the honor of having *five presidents* wanting to see me!

Chapter 6

THE SAWDUST TRAIL

WHEN I LEFT CHARLOTTE, everybody agreed that my arm was gone and never would get right again. Charlotte offered to make me manager of the team if I'd come back the following year. I was at the crossroads. I asked them to give me some time to think it over.

As I arrived at my home in Philadelphia, the girl living next door greeted me with a wonderful smile. I hardly recognized her, she had become so pretty. She had always been "just the kid who lived next door"; but now she was *grown up!* In a surprisingly short time I married that girl.

Giving up baseball—the game I loved so much—was the toughest decision I ever made. Almost every day I changed my mind about it. While this was going on, I discovered that I had one more thing to think over: I found out that we were going to have a baby. That settled it! I decided I'd better take Miller Huggins' advice and quit baseball now, before I got too old to learn something else.

I couldn't go back as a plumber's helper—at eight dollars a week—so I took a job riding a bicycle collecting twenty-five and fifty cents weekly payments for an installment furniture concern. I also managed to get a part-time job coaching the Swarthmore College baseball team—three hundred dollars for three months work each season. During those months I rode my bike like mad to get through collecting in time to catch the 2:30 P.M. train for Swarthmore, about fifteen miles outside the city limits.

For nearly three years I rode that bicycle, barely ekeing out an existence. I wasn't learning much and couldn't see how I'd ever get anywhere else. But there was a surprising event just around the corner that I knew nothing about.

This was the time when Billy Sunday, famous ex-big-league ballplayer, came to Philadelphia on an Evangelistic Campaign. I was not a church-going man but I began reading front page headlines in the papers about thousands of people "hitting the sawdust trail." The whole city was excited.

One evening I read about a well-known preacher who went to Billy and said: "Mr. Sunday, there is a lot of criticism about you. Many people are saying that your conversions don't last." Billy smiled and replied, "Neither does a bath!"

That appealed to me. I thought, *Maybe that's what I need— a bath!*

The next day I knocked off early and rode my bike over to the huge wooden tabernacle on the parkway, erected there just for the Billy Sunday meetings. But when I started to enter, the police stopped me. They said every seat was taken— fifteen thousand of them. "Fire laws would not permit any-more people to be admitted."

An usher, just inside the door, saw them turning me away. I guess he saw the disappointment on my face, because he came right out. He seemed to be looking down at the pants-guards clipped around the bottom of my trousers. I had for-gotten to take them off after I parked my bike. "Officer," said the usher taking hold of my arm, "we've got just one more seat in there for this young man."

With a grand smile he led me up the center aisle. Carloads of sawdust had been spread in the aisles and, to this day, I can feel that sawdust under my feet.

Sure enough . . . there *was* one vacant seat!

Only a few moments after I was seated, Billy Sunday started. I can repeat almost verbatim the story he told:

> One day some years ago I was walking down the street in Chicago with several Chicago White-Sox players. It was Sunday afternoon. We went into a saloon and got tanked up. When we came out, we sat down on the curb. Across the street on the corner, was a small band of men and women playing instruments and singing Gospel Hymns, hymns my Mother used to sing in our log cabin home in Iowa. And I began to sob. Soon a young man came over and said, "We are going down to the Garden, won't you come along with us? I am sure you will enjoy it. You will hear drunkards tell how they have been saved, and girls tell how they have been rescued from the red-light district."
>
> I got up and said to the fellows, "I'm through. I am going to join a *winning* team!—I am going to join up with God!" And I turned my back on them. Some of the fellows laughed, and some mocked me—but one of them gave me encouragement.

Billy Sunday went on to deliver the most inspiring and most exciting message I had ever heard. He told how he gave up a salary of five hundred dollars a month as a ballplayer to work for the Y.M.C.A. for eighty dollars a month. He was a human dynamo! I saw him thump his chest, tear off his coat, collar, and necktie, and throw them on the floor. He leaped up on chairs, flung himself on the floor like a ballplayer sliding into home plate!

Finally, when Billy leaned over the pulpit and began calling for people to come up and take his hand, I was the first one to hit the Sawdust Trail!

When I took his hand, perspiration was running off his face and he was as wet as if he'd just been running the bases for the White-Sox. He smiled and said, "Bless you, my son. Bless you all the days of your life."

I rode home to my family that day with a new kind of courage and faith I'd never known before. I had no idea how or when it would happen, but I knew I wouldn't be riding that bicycle much longer. *Now I was on a winning team!*

... Shortly afterward, during one of the games at Swarthmore, the Chairman of the Athletic Committee, Charles G. Hodge, came down out of the stand and sat on the players' bench alongside of me. For awhile, he just watched to see how the coach directed the team with signals. Later, he asked,

"Frank, what kind of work do you do?" I told him I was just an installment collector. "Come into my office sometime," he suggested, "I'd like to have a talk with you."

It turned out that Mr. Hodge was Secretary of the Fidelity Mutual Life Insurance Company of Philadelphia, a large national company.

I "found time" to go see him the next morning. After asking me a number of questions, he pressed a button and told his secretary to bring in Karl Collings. Mr. Collings was their Philadelphia manager.

Two weeks later I left the house on a Monday morning wearing my Sunday suit. And I wasn't riding a bicycle. I was a Life Insurance Salesman!

4

Chapter 7

I BECOME THE AMAZEMENT OF THE INSURANCE WORLD

Soon after I started out as a salesman, I became the amazement of the insurance world! The company I worked for couldn't understand how it was possible for anyone to make as many calls as they thought I made—and not sell anything!

After ten long, disheartening months, Mr. Colling decided that he knew the answer. He put it right on the line: "I just wasn't cut out to be a salesman." So, my drawing account was cut off. That was the third strike, and I was out.

About this time, an old physical ailment began coming back on me. Its origin sprung, I suppose, from sitting so long on the bench at times with the Cardinals. One day Harry Prutz-man, a semi-retired insurance man in our office, and one of the kindest men I ever knew, told me I looked sick. I confided in him about my condition. He quickly arranged for an old friend of his, the famous surgeon John Deaver, to examine me. Doctor Deaver said he'd operate immediately, and put me into the Lankenau Hospital. He said I'd have to remain there two or three weeks. His fee was almost charity.

Talk about hitting bottom ... I had a double-dose of it.

Lying there in bed after the operation, I was not only in constant pain, but getting lower in spirit than I had ever been in my life. Over and over again I relived those tragic last days in baseball when the accident to my arm forced me out—right at the time when I was really finding myself.

Why? . . . Why? I repeated to myself. There's little Miller Huggins, my old roommate, now manager of the New York Yankees and getting rich! . . . Here I am, at twenty-nine, just a broken down has-been ball player, out of work, getting further into debt every day—a total failure no matter what I do.

My faith about being on a winning team was all gone now.

I became too worried to stay in bed any longer. The fourth day I got up, dressed back of a screen where other patients in the room couldn't see me, and tiptoed down the hall with my little suitcase. The nurses were so busy they never noticed me as I walked slowly down four flights of stairs and slipped out of the crowded hospital. Riding home in a taxicab, I was in great pain. No one was there when I arrived, and it was about all I could do to drag myself upstairs to bed.

A few days later, however, I started out to look for a job, walking the streets answering want-ads. But nobody wanted me. Because of my condition, it didn't seem possible for me to ride a bicycle for awhile, but I became so desperate I tried to get my old job back collecting for Kelly's at eighteen dollars a week. To my utter amazement, even Kelly's turned me down cold!

That afternoon I went out to Swarthmore. I hadn't been out there for ten days. It began to rain so the captain, Jack Riffert, said "Coach, couldn't you take the squad inside and give them a little talk today?" Now I had talked to these fellows individually about batting, fielding, base running, etc., but I never gave a talk to the whole group.

So we all went into a large classroom. A few minutes after I started to talk I suddenly became so terrified I couldn't go on. I rushed out of the room. Out after me came the captain. "What happened, Coach?" he whispered. I told him the truth. "I lost my nerve. I just can't talk to a crowd. I just can't go on." Jack went right back into the room. I didn't wait. I went home. I thought, This is the end! Jack will tell Doc Palmer about this.

The next day I went to Swarthmore expecting to be fired. When I saw Jack, he was fine. I said, "Jack, what did you tell the fellows when you went back into the room?" Grinning, he said, "I just told them the coach had taken some medicine." I could have hugged him, I was so grateful.

Now something happened to me that I've always kept a secret. I turned yellow. I got such a yellow streak I couldn't face a man and ask for a job.

I knew I had to lick this—but quick—or something terrible would happen. I went to the Central Y.M.C.A. and told them about my situation. Next thing I knew I was in a Public Speaking Class that happened to be in session at the time. They assured me it would get me over my trouble, quick. I was introduced to the instructor, Dale Carnegie.

Mr. Carnegie said the course was about halfway through, but another class would be opening in a couple of months and "we would be glad to have you join us then."

"No," I said, "I want to join right now!"

"Wonderful!" Mr. Carnegie smiled and said, as he took my arm, "You're the next speaker!"

He walked me up front and told the class what I said. "Here's a man who is going places!" declared Mr. Carnegie.

Well, after the class heard my speech, they didn't agree with Mr. Carnegie—*and neither did I.*

Then, an amazing thing happened. Mr. Carnegie gave the class an inspiring talk on the power of enthusiasm. He said, "I'm turning gray, and wearing myself out trying to make men wake themselves up and let themselves go!...*to crash through!*"

While he was talking, I kept thinking of Bert Conn, manager of the Johnstown ball team. It seemed like Bert Conn talking to me all over again.

I didn't sleep much that night. I lay awake thinking about how enthusiasm *alone* had raised me from a Class D League to the Major Leagues. The very fault which almost wrecked my career in baseball, had now led me to failure as a salesman. *It was a lesson I had to learn all over again!*

... Can you imagine the surprised expression on Mr. Collings' face—the man who discovered I just wasn't cut out to be a salesman—when he saw me coming into his office the next morning?

This was all I said: "Mr. Collings, I've got an *idea!* Will you give me another chance?"

He studied me for a moment.

He must have seen the fire and excitement in my eyes, for he said: "All right, Bettger, I'll put you back on a drawing account for thirty days. Will that be long enough to prove your idea?"

"It won't take that long!" I assured him.

Chapter 8

"HIT 'EM WITH A BRICK!"

THAT VERY MORNING I made my first call. I felt just like I did before the first game I played in New Haven. "I must show this man the most enthusiastic salesman he has ever seen come in his office!"

Right at the start he told me he wasn't interested. That's where I had always folded up. But now I began to pound my fist; I had to force myself to be enthusiastic. At one point I said to him, "Someday you're going to have an old man on your hands and that old man is going to be *you*. The time to start throwing forward passes to him is right *now!*" As I said 'throwing forward passes,' I swung my hand overhead like a football player throwing a forward pass. Every minute I expected him to stop me and ask if I was all right. But he never did, except to ask questions. Finally, he *bought!* When he wrote out his check paying the whole first year in advance, I felt like letting out a great yell.

I was so excited I rushed right back to the insurance company office—deliberately passing by Kelly's on my way—and laid the application and check in front of Mr. Collings on his desk. The commission on that sale was enough to cover my advance for the entire thirty days he had allotted me. He was astonished. "How did you do it?" he asked. As I told him the story his eyes popped and he said, "I want you to repeat this sale at our agency meeting next Monday morning."

That night I think I must have been the most triumphant man in Philadelphia. My fear was all gone now. I knew I had it licked. I was a new Frank Bettger . . . and I knew why!

One of the most unforgettable talks I ever made to any audience was the one I made a few nights later, when I told the public speaking class I had gone back to the insurance company, asked them to give me another trial; and how I had sold the first man I called on by putting the same enthusiasm into my sales talk as I had put into baseball.

I told them why this was one of the biggest triumphs in my life; that only a few days before I was a total and absolute failure, out of work and couldn't get a job, couldn't even ask for one. Mr. Carnegie and the whole class seemed as excited and happy about it as I was.

After class, I was surprised when one of the members, Horace Groskin, a successful real estate man, came to me and suggested that I join him in offering our services as speakers to the "Four-Minute-Men." The United States had been drawn into World War I. The Government had created an organization of speakers, and named them "Four-Minute-Men." They were sent around to mass meetings, industrial plants, churches, theatres and so forth, to deliver various messages from the government. Also to sell War Bonds. Mr. Groskin said it was impossible for them to get enough speakers.

I said: "Mr. Groskin, I have never made a speech in my life, except in this class."

"Neither have I," said he; "but I've heard a few of these

speakers, and they're not so hot. Let's try it. It will be mighty good experience."

I had been reading a three by five inch card each morning I'd stuck to our bathroom mirror:

RULE ONE TO CONQUER FEAR
Do the thing you fear to do; and keep on doing it, until you get a record of successful experiences behind you.

I thought, "Here's an opportunity to put that rule into action; and at the same time do my share in the war effort."

The next morning, Horace Groskin and I went to the Four-Minute-Men Headquarters, and offered our services.

They started me off by sending me to small neighborhood movie theatres. I thought I'd black out the first night. Then one night, they assigned me to a fairly large movie house in West Philadelphia. Riding out there on a trolley, I happened to meet John Dennis Mahoney, a professor and well-known speaker and poet. I had heard him speak one time at the Y.M.C.A. I introduced myself and asked him for a bit of advice. I explained that the movie theatres always put me on between shows during the change of audience; that there was so much noise and confusion, nobody heard my talk. I asked the professor how I could overcome this situation.

"HIT 'EM WITH A BRICK!" was his surprising advice.

"How do you mean?" I asked.

"Say something startling."

He gave me this example : "During a very hot summer with the temperature ninety-eight degrees, Henry Ward Beecher, the famous preacher, came into his church one Sunday morning through the front entrance. He walked slowly down the center aisle mopping his face and neck with a large handkerchief.

When he reached the pulpit, he turned, looked out over the
congregation, still mopping his brow, and said: 'It's a hell of
a hot day, isn't it?' He paused a moment, then continued:
'That's what I heard a man say out front as I was coming into
church!' The congregation forgot all about the heat then and
listened with great interest to his sermon."

When I arrived at the movie theatre, I was still trying to
figure out how I could "hit 'em with a brick." I took a seat
directly in front of the steps leading onto the stage. The very
instant the main picture ended, I leaped onto the stage, threw
my fist high over my head and yelled: "TO HELL WITH THE
KAISER!"

It worked! Everybody stopped as though they'd been shot
at! So I continued: "That's what I heard a man say out front
just as I was coming into the theatre ... but what are *you*
doing to put him there?"

I went on with my four-minute message and they all listened.

I was gaining more courage now. So the next day, I called
on the Manager of the Texaco Company. I'd been afraid to call
on him before. His name had been given to me months previously by a friend of mine, a clerk in the Texaco office. "Don't
tell him I sent you," warned my friend, "he'd fire me."

A secretary ushered me into the manager's office. When I
introduced myself he blew up:

"I'm not seeing any insurance salesmen today! I've been out
of the office for two months with a nervous breakdown. Last
night, my wife said: 'Come on, let's go around the corner to
the movie. It will do you good.' So I went along with her.
Just as I sat down in my seat, some crazy idiot leaped up on
the stage and yelled in the loudest voice I ever heard: 'TO
HELL WITH THE KAISER!' I thought I would die."

I tried not to laugh, but it was so unexpected, I looked at him, grinned, then burst right out!

"What is so funny about it?" he roared.

As soon as I could control myself, I admitted I was that man. Up he jumped from behind the desk, his face purple with rage —pointing to the door: "GET THE HELL OUT OF HERE AND DON'T YOU EVER COME BACK!"

And I never did.

A few days later I was in the Four-Minute-Men Headquarters waiting for an assignment to go up to a small industrial plant and talk to the workers during their lunch hour. Suddenly, a phone call came in from Washington that Charles Schwab, Administrator of the War Board, had been delayed by an emergency meeting and couldn't address the 16,000 employees of the E. G. Budd Manufacturing Company that day. At the time, Charles Schwab, with the exception of the President of the United States, was the most talked of man in the nation.

I heard one of the men say: "What in heaven's name will we do?"

Somebody else replied: "Get another man. Get your best speaker to replace Schwab."

"But we haven't time. It's too late. The employees are already gathering outside of Budd's to hear Mr. Schwab.

The next thing I knew I was speeding up Broad Street in a beautiful new open Cadillac, streamers flying from it, sirens blowing, motorcycle police riding before and aft. Several city officials were with us, but nobody bothered even to ask my name. All traffic was stopped to let us go straight through at sixty miles an hour.

When we arrived at the Budd plant, a wounded veteran was up on the decorated stand, speaking. He had just been brought back from France, one arm gone, face still in bandages. He told some harrowing stories of what our boys were going through "Over There."

Then I was introduced by Mr. Leo I. Heintz, vice-president of the Budd company. He explained that Mr. Schwab had been unavoidably detained in Washington, and that Mr. Bettger, one of the Four-Minute-Men, would speak in Mr. Schwab's place.

I guess I was too big a let-down for that crowd. When I finished, I felt like I had struck out in the ninth inning with the bases full. As I came down off the stand, after the affair was over and the workers were returning to the plant, a man walked up to me and shook my hand. You'd never guess who it was. It was "Bowels" McCarthy, the park sparrow who played in that game with McDaniel's Saloon the day we beat "Reds" Donahue's Saloon. He said politely, "That was pretty good, Betch."

I said, "Bowels, are you working here at Budd's?"

He grinned and said, "Yeah, the war finally caught up wid me."

It took a World War to make him go to work!

When I went out to look for the handsome streamered Cadillac which had brought me there, it was gone. They hadn't bothered to wait to take me back into town.

I walked down to the corner and took a trolley back. On the way I got to thinking: "No wonder I struck out with the bases full. This is more ridiculous than the time I had pinch-hit for Miller Huggins at the Polo Grounds with Christy Mathewson pitching. Here I am, a poor dub salesman on a $35.00 weekly drawing account. Suddenly they pull me off the bench and race me up to pinch-hit for Charles Schwab, president of Bethlehem Steel, the only man in the world to draw a salary of a million dollars a year. How ridiculous can you get!"

I took out my pencil and figured it up. Why, Schwab's salary amounted to more every three hours than my drawing account added up to for an entire year!

Rule Number One to Conquer Fear

The most important rule I ever found to conquer fear and develop courage and self-confidence is:

> DO THE THING YOU FEAR TO DO:
> AND KEEP ON DOING IT UNTIL
> YOU GET A RECORD OF
> SUCCESSFUL EXPERIENCES
> BEHIND YOU.

If I hadn't learned this rule, and forced myself to *apply it* by enlisting as a Four-Minute-Man, I would have missed one of the most rewarding experiences in my life—learning to speak in public.

"Fear to do ill, and you need fear nought else."
                                                    B. FRANKLIN

Chapter 9

THE SMUTS STORY

SHORTLY AFTER PINCH-HITTING for Charles Schwab, I met Horace Groskin, the man who urged me to join the "Four-Minute Men" with him. Groskin had quickly become one of their star speakers. When I told him about my "striking out" for the famous million-dollar-a-year Schwab, he laughed so hard, it actually hurt him.

But Horace Groskin then gave me an idea that made an immediate difference in my speaking. He told me the real secret of his success in selling more War Bonds than any other Four-Minute-Man in Philadelphia—was in telling stories. Stories of actual happenings "behind the lines," as well as happenings "out on the firing lines."

One of the stories I used the very next day at a small industrial plant during their lunch hour. Twenty-six employees sat up on the machinery. Before I started, I drew a heavy white chalkline across the floor in front of the machines. Standing on a bench facing them, I said, "Men, I'm only going to talk four minutes. I want to tell you a story...

"Just when the Allies had their backs against the wall, the coal miners in South Wales called a strike. Result? No coal

for the Navy, or the factories that were producing war muni-
tions. It was a paralyzing blow. The reserve supply of coal
would be exhausted in ten days!

"General Jan Christian Smuts of South Africa, one of Great
Britain's most heroic leaders, was rushed up to address the
miners. I'll never forget the story. Here it is—the General's
own words:

> " 'I arrived at Cardiff early the next morning. I went
> immediately to the coal fields. Practically the whole road
> from Cardiff to the fields was lined with strikers. Finally,
> I arrived at Tonypandy, center of the strike area. A vast
> crowd gathered, numbering thousands of angry strikers.
> I said, "Gentlemen, I come from far away, as you know.
> I have come to do my bit in this war, and I am going to
> talk to you about this trouble. But I have heard in my
> country that the Welsh are among the greatest singers in
> the world, and before I start, I want you to sing to me
> one of the songs of your people."
>
> " 'Immediately, someone in the rear of the huge mass
> struck up the "Land of My Fathers." Every soul present
> joined in the song, and when they had finished, they just
> stood, and I could see that the thing was over, the atmos-
> phere was less electrified. I said, "Well, Gentlemen, it is
> not necessary for me to say much here tonight. You know
> what has happened on the Western Front. You know
> your comrades in their tens of thousands are risking their
> lives. You know that the Front is not only in France, but
> that the Front is just as much right here as anywhere
> else."
>
> " 'That was all I said, I spoke only a few minutes. I
> went on to the next meeting, and repeated the same thing
> there. Late that night, I took the train back to London.
> Members of the Cabinet met me and exclaimed, "What
> has happened, all the men are back at work!"
>
> " 'I said "Is that so? It is news to me." ' "

When I finished, I followed Horace Groskin's instructions precisely. I said: "Well, men, you know that the Front is just as much here as it is over there. How many of you are willing to cross the line and sign up for a War Bond?"

One man quickly jumped off a machine and crossed the line . . . and all the other twenty-five immediately followed.

I continued using that story until I knew it practically verbatim. Its effect always seemed like magic.

After the war ended, for two years I worked as a "bird dog," digging up prospects for one of the nation's great salesmen, Clayton M. Hunsicker. I soon learned one of the important secrets of his success. He sold largely by telling stories! He was a master of the human interest story.

I asked him about this one day. He said, "Selling, in a large sense, *is* story-telling, for you are telling the story about your 'goods,' you are putting your ideas into *action*. It's dramatization!"

I said, "I am amazed at the amount of time busy business men give you. They sit there listening with rapt attention, and seem to forget all about time."

"The secret," Mr. Hunsicker explained, "is that I always make sure my story fits *their* situation, or problem. That's why they are so anxious to hear the solution."

This method of story-telling became an enormous help to me as a salesman, and later in lecturing and writing. I've also found it equally important to get the *other person* to tell stories. One or two tactful questions usually does it. For example:

"How did you happen to get started in the carpet manufacturing business, Mr. Doerr?"

This question always seems to please men. I believe there is nothing you can possibly say to an individual that would be half as interesting to *him* as the things he would love to tell you about himself, and it tells *me* a lot about him that I would like to know, but might hesitate to ask him about.

I have learned a lot about life and a lot about people—by listening to these romantic stories. I find them exciting and inspiring—an education in itself.

Part Two

HOW I CHANGED MY LINE-UP

An Idea, discovered by one of the World's most honored Scientists, the BIG IDEA *which was to revolutionize my entire life.*

Chapter 10

FRANKLIN'S SECRET OF SUCCESS

Holding a book up one night in Class, Dale Carnegie said he would like every one of us to read it, and reread it, several times. It was *The Autobiography of Benjamin Franklin.* Mr. Carnegie said it was one of the most famous and inspiring books ever written.

He told us Franklin had been a poor boy—started working at ten years of age after only two years of formal schooling; that when just a small printer in Philadelphia, badly in debt, he hit upon an idea which he thought would make him a better business man. And that it was *this idea* which raised Ben Franklin from failure to success, made him rich, and made him one of the wisest men who ever walked this earth!

I was amazed when Mr. Carnegie explained how simple the idea was. *Anyone* could use it!

Franklin devised a plan based on thirteen principles, and annexed to each one a short precept which fully expressed the extent he gave to its meaning. In a little book—which he carried with him at all times—he allotted a page to each principle, and recorded his successes and failures. He didn't try to prac-

57

tice them all at once, but determined to give a week's strict attention to each one successively. Since he wanted thirteen principles, and there were fifty-two weeks in a year, he hoped to practice each principle four times a year. In devoting a full week to one principle, Franklin soon discovered that he was developing a great power of concentration—the ability to think things through!

A half century later, near the end of his amazing life, Franklin wrote that to this one idea he owed his success and happiness. "I hope therefore, that some of my descendants may follow the example and reap the benefit."

To me, this sounded fantastic. Why, I had never even heard of this *Autobiography* and I knew almost nothing of Benjamin Franklin,—except that he flew a kite! But when we found out that the Y.M.C.A. had arranged to get these books for us far below retail price, I thought there must be something to it. So I bought one. It only cost me a dollar. What could I lose?

While Mr. Carnegie was talking, a crazy idea hit me that only an ex-ballplayer would get, which drew a parallel with this plan of Franklin's.

When my old roommate, Miller Huggins, was appointed manager of the New York Yankees, it was a losing team. Huggins' first move was to change the line-up of the Yankees, with new players in almost every position . . . men like Babe Ruth, Lou Gehrig, Bob Meusel, Waite Hoyt, and others. That new line-up lifted the Yankees from failure to success. Within three years, they climbed from last place to first place—and the Yankees became the American League Champions!

"Why that's exactly what happened to Ben Franklin," I said to myself. "Ben was playing a losing game in the printing business. He merely decided to change his line-up."

I determined to give Ben's plan a chance—thirteen weeks of

it. The "line-up" I chose was like Franklin's. At first, however, I applied it just to selling. Of Franklin's thirteen principles, I chose six, substituting seven others which I thought would be more helpful to me in my business. I lined up 3 x 5 inch index cards, and printed in large letters one principle on each of them. Then, gradually, over the years, I adapted my principles to serve me for everyday living, as Ben Franklin's served him.

I thought, "Changing my line-up is like adopting the Yankee system: put the best players in each position and let 'em win for you!" I made a game out of it. It was fun, it was exciting. It was like being back in baseball all over again.

I carried out the idea just as Franklin did, giving one week's strict attention to each principle.

I soon found myself gaining more confidence. I knew I was going places now. As each week progressed, I could see it in my business, and in my life.

I got so excited about the plan, I just had to talk with somebody. I had been keeping it a secret, just as Franklin had, I was so afraid of being ridiculed by my family and my friends.

But I could tell Miller Huggins. Huggins would understand, because he did the same thing himself, with the Yankees' line-up. And it was "Hug" who advised me to get out of baseball and get into something else before it was too late.

So, now that I had completed my first cycle of thirteen weeks, I hopped on a train one Saturday morning with my thirteen cards in my pocket—"Pocket Reminders," I called them —and was on my way to New York to see Miller Huggins.

Chapter 11

THE SECRET INGREDIENT

To my great joy, soon after I arrived in New York this day, I found myself sitting alongside my old roommate in the Clubhouse at the famous Polo Grounds. This was before the Yankee Stadium had been built. I said, "Hug, I have adopted the same system in my business that you've set up—the Yankee System."

"What do you mean?" he asked curiously.

I told him how I was lying in the hospital, broke and out of a job; how I began thinking about his going to New York as their new manager, changing the Yankees' line-up and how they became a winning team.

I said, "At first, I was bitter, getting lower in spirit than I had ever been in my life. But later, when I thought it over, I became inspired by what you had done, Hug. I decided that's what I needed, a new 'line-up'."

I showed him the thirteen 3 x 5 inch pocket reminders I had with me. Then, in a few words, I told Hug how I had drawn a parallel between his plan and Franklin's, and how it was affecting my life.

I watched his face as he glanced briefly over each card. There were only two big things about Huggins—his big mouth and his brain. Handing the cards back to me, he registered absolutely no reaction to them. Getting up, he said, "I've got to get out on the field now, Frank. We're pulling off a surprise exhibition before the game today you might be interested in. Stop back and see me after the game."

Now these were the days when the immortal Babe Ruth was rolling up his unapproached lifetime world's record, hitting seven hundred and twenty-nine home runs, including fifteen in the World Series. Because of him a new type of fan was appearing at the Polo Grounds. This was the fan who didn't know where first base was, but had heard of Babe Ruth and wanted to see him hit a home run. The Babe had become a national idol.

Just before the game started, out walked Babe to the home plate. He took his position in the batter's box and one of the Yankees' pitchers began throwing balls with great speed up to Ruth. Babe took his magnificent swings, and to the delight of some 50,000 ball fans, drove a number of balls over the fence.

One ball carried over the 441-foot mark in deep center field. Many people in that crowd hadn't seen the King of Swat often enough to realize his tremendous driving power. Now they thrilled to it. Even the players on both teams stood up and applauded with the crowd!

But then came the big surprise Huggins had tipped me off to. A beautiful young girl walked out to the home plate and was introduced to the crowd. She was Joyce Wethered from England, and she had just won the British Women's Open Golf Championship. Joyce had become recognized as the world's greatest woman golfer. As this lovely young miss shook hands with the 6 ft. 2 inches, 210 lb. Babe Ruth, she looked more like a child.

Only a couple of people in the stadium had any idea of the astonishing feat they were about to witness. Not even the Babe knew.

Joyce stepped into the batter's box, stooped down and placed a golf ball on a tiny wooden tee which she pressed into the ground. The Yankees' bat-boy handed her a golf club, and she took a couple of easy practice swings. Then she drove that ball so high and far over the right-field fence that people could scarcely believe their own eyes. Again, Joyce teed up a ball and drove that one far over the left-field fence. But now came the real payoff. She teed up again, faced the 441 ft. sign in center field and drove the ball so high over the sign that it went over the clubhouse roof! . . . It still may be traveling somewhere in the world, because the last the crowd saw of that ball it was headed full speed for the Harlem River, which waters soon flow out into the Atlantic Ocean. . .

After the game when I met Huggins again, he asked, "How did you like Joyce Wethered outdriving Babe Ruth, the 'mightiest slugger of them all?'"

I said, "That was one of the most amazing things I ever saw. What's the answer?"

"The answer," said Huggins grinning, "is that golf balls are constructed to drive twice as far as a baseball. The secret is in the ingredient."

Then Miller Huggins exploded an idea on me that was DYNAMITE. He said: "Frank, when Bert Conn tied a can to you in Johnstown, there was a secret ingredient in that can. That ingredient took you up to the Big Leagues in baseball. Later, it took you back into the insurance business after you failed, and you started making sales. If you will apply this same magic ingredient to *every one of those thirteen principles* you showed me on the cards, you could become one of the greatest life insurance men in America!"

That idea electrified me! That was just the spark I needed to *set the plan on fire*. It was Bert Conn who put the stick of dynamite in the can. But it took Miller Huggins to *explode* it!

1. Enthusiasm
2. Order: Self-Organization
3. Others
4. Questions
5. Silence; Listen
6. Resolution
7. Frugality
8. Sincerity
9. Praise vs. Criticism
10. Health
11. Happiness
12. Humility
13. Faith

Chapter 12

HOW I ADDED TEN YEARS TO MY LIFE

WHEN I ARRIVED HOME late that night from New York, I was the most excited man in Philadelphia. It had been a lot of fun meeting and talking with many of those great Yankee ball-players, including Babe Ruth . . . but Miller Huggins had exploded a BIG IDEA. The idea had never occurred to me, but Hug saw it in a flash.

I set my alarm clock to go off the following morning at six A.M., an hour-and-a-half earlier than usual. What better way, I thought, could I start putting this dynamite into every one of the thirteen principles, than the way Franklin did? Ben discovered that early risers—on the average—live to an older age, and are usually more successful in life. So, when he changed his line-up, he began getting up at five o'clock in the morning. In addition to adding two hours a day to his life, he believed this increased the length of his life. Franklin lived to be eighty-four—thirty years beyond the average in those times!

My poor mother had to get up at five A.M. every day to take care of five little children; took in washing and ironing

besides going out to do a day's work for years. If hard work
would kill anyone, my mother could never have survived to age
fifty. But she lived to enjoy good health until just before her
death at eighty-three.

So I joined the Six O'clock Club.

At first, I had trouble getting out of bed at such an early
hour, but I caught onto a simple little trick: after a good stretch,
I stuck one foot out from under the covers, then my leg; now
the other leg, and the next thing I knew, I was up!

Soon, I began getting up at six o'clock automatically, and
I didn't need the alarm at all.

It would be almost impossible to exaggerate how important
that extra hour-and-a-half in the morning was to me. I found
it the most exhilarating hour of the day. My mind was clear,
the house was quiet. An hour of that time I used for reading
and studying a Tax and Insurance Service I had subscribed to
and was paying for on the installment plan, but didn't have
time for. I soon caught up with the course and began to gain
so much confidence from my newly acquired knowledge that
I determined to go on and try to become one of the best
informed men in my business. This was the same guy who
only a few months before thought he was licked.

The other half hour in the morning I reviewed the work
I had planned for the day; then silent prayer for enthusiasm
to perform the resolutions of the day. If I had any time left
over, I read some inspirational material or other articles of
interest from magazines I would bring home from the office.

One morning whose picture should I see on the cover of a
magazine but Charles Schwab, the million-dollar-a-year-man
I had pinch-hit for at the Budd Manufacturing plant. The story
told how an efficiency expert had given Schwab an idea which

helped him make One Hundred Million Dollars. The heart of the story was an interview between Mr. Schwab and Ivy Lee, the pioneer for big business. Lee operated an efficiency firm in New York City. His clients included John D. Rockefeller, J. P. Morgan, the DuPonts, Pennsylvania Railroad, and other giant corporations.

In this interview, Lee briefly outlined his organization's service, and ended modestly by saying: "With our service, you'll know how to manage better."

"Hell!" said Schwab, "I'm not managing as well now as I know how. What we need around here is not more 'knowing,' but more 'doing'; not knowledge, but action. If you can give us something to pep us up to do the things we already know we ought to do, I'll gladly listen to you and pay you anything you ask."

"Fine," answered Lee. "I can give you something in twenty minutes that will step up your action and doing at least fifty per cent."

"Okay," said Schwab, "let's have it. I've got just about that much time before I leave to catch a train."

Lee handed Mr. Schwab a blank note-sheet from his pocket and said: "Write on this paper the six most important tasks you have to do tomorrow." That took about three minutes. "Now," said Lee, "number them in the order of their importance." Schwab took five minutes for that. "Now," said Lee, "put this paper in your pocket and the first thing tomorrow morning look at item one and start working on it until it is finished. Then tackle item two in the same way; then item three, and so on. Do this until quitting time. Don't be concerned if you have only finished one or two. You'll be working on the more important ones. The others can wait. If you can't finish them all by this method, you couldn't have with any other method either; and without some system, you'd probably not even decided which was the most important.

"Do this every working day. After you've convinced yourself of the worth of this system, have your men try it. Try it as long as you wish, and then send me a check for what you think it is worth."

The whole interview lasted about thirty minutes. Several weeks later, Schwab sent Lee a check for $25,000 with a letter saying the lesson was the most profitable from a money standpoint, that he had ever learned. In five years, this plan was largely responsible for turning the unknown Bethlehem Steel Company into the biggest independent steel producer in the world! And it helped make Charles Schwab a hundred million dollars, and the best known steel man alive.

Was I astounded! A million-dollar-a-year man saying that "Order and Self-organization" had been his greatest problem— and the solution so simple. Yet, Franklin had said practically the same thing.

... Eight years as a professional baseball player seemed to have left me one of the world's worst self-organizers. So, I combined Schwab's system with Franklin's, planning the entire week ahead.

I soon found enormous advantages to this. At first, I didn't know how to start, but finally got it through my thick head that I must take more time for planning. Schwab made it compulsory for his men to set aside a period at the end of each day to plan their next day's tasks ... and included himself in the order too. So, I set aside every Friday morning and made it compulsory.

Franklin's life was so inspiring, I wanted to study more about him. He spent a couple of hours a day reading and studying to make up for his lack of education. I didn't see how I could find any more time for reading; but I bought another copy of his *Autobiography*, an inexpensive, second-hand edition, tore out a few pages each morning, and tucked them in my pocket. At odd moments during the day, riding on a trolley car, train, waiting outside of a man's office, I read those pages. Waiting time was no longer a dead loss.

Later, I decided to test the "fifteen-minutes-a-day" installment reading idea of Charles Eliot, famous president of Harvard University. I invested in a set of those wonderful books *The Five Foot Book Shelf*. I also had to pay for them on the installment plan.

Immediately after dinner each evening, I grabbed one of those books and began reading. It was only a self-starter. At the end of half an hour, I had to force myself to stop. That still left plenty of time for my family, the newspaper, or anything else I felt like doing for the remainder of the evening.

Reading those books only a short time each evening, opened up a whole new world of knowledge to me, and was the closest I ever came to a college education.

During all these weeks of operating on my new line-up, I had been keeping records. They were accurate, for I had put the figures down every day religiously. I was soon able to attach an exact value to my time. One Friday morning, while studying these records, I discovered that each call I made netted me $2.30! Every call I made, regardless of whether I saw the man or not, put $2.30 down in my pocket.

Now, a startling idea hit me: I'm going to hire a private secretary!

This seemed fantastic. It scared me at first to think of it. Frank Bettger having a secretary! My own boss, Karl Collings, didn't have a private secretary, even the biggest producer in our Company didn't have a secretary.

I was plenty scared. Yet, there were the facts. Facts based on actual records. I would need to make only ten additional calls a week, and I'd have the advantages of a secretary free— absolutely free.

Right at this time, there was a fine young man named Russell Mathias calling on a girl in our office. They were engaged to be married. Russell had just returned from military service. He was still in uniform when I heard that he could type, take dictation, and do general office work; I talked to him about my idea. We agreed on a salary and he took the job. I said, "Russell, I can afford to pay you this much now, and in time probably much more, if you can do one job." He said: "What's that, Mr. Bettger?" I said: *"Keep me out of the office four days a week."* I'll phone you each afternoon at two o'clock for any messages; dictate notes; give you calls to be entered on next week's schedule, and so forth. We can accomplish about everything that we could if I came into the office. Fridays, I will spend in the office with you, organizing and planning the entire week ahead."

Well! When Mr. Collings, Mr. Hunsicker, and other men in the office saw Russell Mathias sitting at my desk, and found out that he was Frank Bettger's private secretary, word got around, Bettger, the green, blundering dub who only a short time before had his drawing account cut off, had gone completely "off his rocker"!

The following Friday, when I came into the office, Mr. Collings began questioning me like I needed psychiatric treatment. I pulled out my records and showed him the facts.

In a surprisingly short time, both Mr. Collings and Mr. Hunsicker had private secretaries of their own. Only theirs were much prettier than Russell Mathias!

If you want to know whether you're going to be a success in your business, or whatever your calling in life may be, the test is easy: *Can you organize and control your time?* If not, drop out, for you will surely *fail!* You may not think so, but you will fail as surely as you live . . .

If you want to enjoy one of the greatest luxuries in life—the luxury of having enough time—time to play; time to rest; time to *think things through;* time to get things done and know you have done them to the best of your ability, remember there is only *one* way: Take enough *time* to think and plan things in the order of their importance. Your life will take on a new zest. You will add years to your life—and more *life* to your years!

Let all your things have their places; let each part of your business have its time. . . . FRANKLIN

Chapter 13

IT WAS A MIRACLE

Now what happened? Was I "off my rocker," like they said? Well, at the end of that year, I stood ninety-second among all the salesmen in the company, and I'd had a secretary to take care of all the paper work—for free!

The next year I had completed four more cycles, or courses, as Franklin called it, and I stood 13th.

A year later I woke up in a strange hotel room in Atlanta, Georgia, to hear somebody pounding like murder on the door and an unfamiliar voice calling out an old familiar refrain: "Frank. Get up! THE PRESIDENT WANTS TO SEE YOU!"

I nearly fell flat on my face getting up from a sound sleep, and wondered just where I was. But suddenly I came to, and remembered that something wonderful had happened!

I was to be honored this morning at a meeting for having won the "President's Cup"—for being first among all the representatives in the company for the entire year.

Here I was getting a *cup* instead of a *can* this time. It all seemed like a miracle.

It was a miracle. Only four years before, at twenty-nine,

a complete failure, in the depths of despair, I had given up all hope of ever becoming a salesman. Now here I was, the same man, on the first leg of a tour around the country with the top executives of my company—the same company that had cut me off the payroll—attending their regional conventions as their principal speaker! To me, this was like a guy who had a can tied on him four years before, now pitching the big game in a World Series!

The Company was paying further honor to "this man who came back," by attaching a sticker at the top of every application form with his picture on it. Over the picture it read: BETTGER MONTH. The Fidelity had never done this before for any salesman. And they wouldn't be doing it now for me if I were anything like a super-salesman. They were honoring me only because I was just an ordinary salesman, who had raised himself from failure to success. And their instructions to me were: "Simply tell at those meetings precisely what you did, the ideas that lifted you out of the ranks of failure, what those ideas did for you, and will do for anyone who will apply them."

... My proudest thought and greatest thrill was that my wonderful Mother had lived to see her sickly little boy who doctors said she wouldn't be able to raise, grow up to make something of the life she worked so hard to save.

I mailed her a copy of the "Fidelity Field Man," the company's monthly publication, featuring me on the cover.

I also mailed a copy to Miller Huggins, enclosing a note: "Dear Hug, here's what that Dynamite you exploded did for your old roommate! I shall be eternally grateful to you. Enthusiastically yours . . . PEP BETCHER."

Huggins must have phoned our company's Head Office in Philadelphia because when we arrived at the St. Charles Hotel

in New Orleans a few days later, there was a telegram awaiting
me—the most thrilling telegram I ever remember getting from
anyone.

> CONGRATULATIONS! YOUR REMARKABLE
> ACHIEVEMENT HAS INSPIRED THE WHOLE
> YANKEE TEAM. MY TALK TO THEM IN THE
> CLUBHOUSE TODAY WAS ABOUT YOU. THEY
> HAVE AGREED TO DOUBLE THEIR ENTHUSI-
> ASM DURING THE BALANCE OF THE SEASON
> . . . DID YOU EVER THANK BERT CONN?
> MILLER HUGGINS

I began to feel myself choking up. Those last words in
Huggins' telegram: DID YOU EVER THANK BERT CONN?—shook
me all the way down to my shoetops! In all the years that had
gone by, it never occurred to me that I should thank Bert Conn!
Yet it was true . . . *he had helped change my life*.

I determined to make a trip to Johnstown as soon as I got
back to Philadelphia.

But the tour I was on kept me away several weeks. When
I arrived back home, I found myself snowed under with work
that had piled up. I kept putting off and putting off my trip to
see Bert Conn. It wasn't until considerable time later, at a
large meeting I was addressing in New York City, that a badly
handicapped man, crippled from polio, came up to me on
crutches at the close of my talk. His name was Leo J. Buettner.
Leo was from Johnstown, Pennsylvania! He was one of the
most dynamic men I ever met, and had more enthusiasm than
any dozen of the other men who shook hands with me. I had
mentioned "Point Stadium" in my talk, and having played with
Johnstown.

Leo was a very successful insurance man in Johnstown, and

his office was directly opposite Point Stadium. To my utter amazement, he told me that Bert Conn was the owner of a big trucking business right in Philadelphia.

As soon as I got home, I looked it up in the phone book. Sure enough, there it was!—on Frankford Avenue in the big manufacturing section. I didn't phone. I wanted this to be a complete surprise. I hopped in my car and drove right up there. As I walked into a huge garage filled with big trucks, a tall, husky man stepped up to me and asked if there was something he could do for me. I think I was almost as nervous as I had been when Bert fired me in Johnstown. "This must be Bert," I thought. "Same size. About the right age."

"Is this Bert Conn?" I asked.

"No," the man replied, "Mr. Conn is not here now."

"Do you expect him today?"

"No, he won't be in. He's sick."

I said, "Look, I'm an old friend of his, played ball with him years ago in Johnstown. I've got something to tell Bert that might make him feel better. Do you suppose I could go to see him?"

"I don't think so. He's in the Chestnut Hill Hospital, and nobody is allowed to see him except his wife."

I showed the man Miller Huggins' telegram that I received in New Orleans, that year the Yankees won their first pennant. I said, "Maybe it would do Bert a lot of good to know what he had done to help my life."

"I'll call Mrs. Conn tonight," he promised, "and tell her about it."

But I never saw Bert Conn alive again. He passed away two days later.

I had waited too long.

Chapter 14

"PUFF STUFF"

An enthusiastic young English physician named Roger Bannister one day astounded the sports world by running the mile in 3:59.4. Never before had any human being run the mile in four minutes. For centuries, it was believed to be impossible.

Now look what happened! Roger Bannister's boundless enthusiasm was contagious. It had removed the mental block —the belief that "it couldn't be done." Only six weeks later, John Landy of Australia broke Bannister's world record by racing the mile in 3:58!

Within four years, what "couldn't be done" was done nineteen times by nine different runners. Herb Elliott, the twenty-year-old Australian clerk ran the mile under four minutes— ten times! And, on August 6, 1958, the amazing Herb Elliott established a new world record: he raced the mile in 3:54.5!

Elliott said: "You get bloody sick of training, but that's when one runner proves himself better than the others. Anyone can do it when he's enthusiastic."

I know what happened to these men. I know, because it happened to me... One of the saddest days in my life was the day Bert Conn fired me in Johnstown. Yet, when I arrived in New Haven only three weeks later, I couldn't throw a ball any better, or catch or hit better. I didn't know any more about baseball than I did before. I didn't have anything in New Haven that I didn't have in Johnstown—that is, nothing but the determination to act enthusiastic.

Years later, after failing completely as a salesman, when I went back to the insurance company ten days after being fired and asked the manager for another chance, I didn't have anything then that I didn't have before when they cut me off the payroll—that is, nothing but the determination to act enthusiastic! And I began to sell!

What did it? Enthusiasm alone did it; nothing but enthusiasm!

A number of years ago I was in Columbia, South Carolina, when I read in the newspapers that a murder trial was to be conducted there by a famous southern Judge, beginning that morning.

This trial had made the front-page headlines of all the newspapers throughout the nation. I had never witnessed a murder trial, and decided to go over and listen in.

As I crossed the street onto the beautiful courthouse grounds, there were the usual tents and stands set up by fakers who always follow circuit judges around the circuit. Well, one of these fellows stole the show. There was some kind of excitement in his voice that drew everybody down to his stand, including me. He was wearing a racetrack-checkered suit, red suspenders, a brown derby hat, and puffing on a great big cigar. I saw him make thirty sales in five minutes. Here was his sales talk, just about as he gave it, delivered with the most exciting enthusiasm of any salesman I ever heard:

"LADIES AND GENTLEMEN AND FELLOW CITIZENS, MY NAME IS PUFFSTUFF! PHYSICIAN AND SURGEON TO THE GREAT AND MIGHTY KHAN KAHOO, EMPEROR OF CHINA! I was converted to Christianity during the reign of the late Lord MacAriel, left that country and came to this, which might be counted one of the greatest blessings that ever happened to America!

"I brought with me the following insatiable, never-to-be-matched medicines, the first of which is called Prairie-Random-Ratskinium, from Wang-de-Wang-Wang, one drop of which, placed upon the gums, if any of you are so unfortunate as to lose your teeth, *will cause a new set to sprout forth like mushrooms from a hotbed!*—or, if any lady is troubled with that painful exploitation called a beard, one application will remove it with greater ease than a barber's razor! I also brought with me that Wonderful, Grand Elliptical, Ecclesiastical Panacure-all or Nervous Cordial that cures ALL diseases incidental to humanity! . . . I am also very celebrated in the cure of eyes. The late Emperor of China was so unfortunate as to lose the sight of both his eyes by cataract. I very dexterously removed the eyes of His Majesty, and after anointing the sockets to a peculiar degree of illumination, placed therein two eyes from the head of a living lion, which not only completely restored his vision, but rendered him dreadful to all enemies and beholders!

". . . Now, ladies and gentlemen, I don't wish to brag on myself, because he who brags on himself is worse than a hedgehog; but I am not only the greatest physician and philosopher of the age; I am also the greatest genius known to mankind!

"But as I said before, I don't wish to brag on myself, but

I would like to read to you a list of a few of the cures that have come to me from the many thousands who have benefited by this WONDERFUL, GRAND ELIPTICAL, ECCLESIASTI-CAL, PANACURE-ALL, or NERVOUS CORDIAL, that none of you should be such fools as to be sick at all! Allow me to read just a few of them:

ATLANTA, GEORGIA: "Stoned to death in a street riot" ... CURED with one bottle!

CHICAGO, ILLINOIS: "Boiled to death in a soap factory" ... CURED with one bottle!

PORTLAND, OREGON: "Cut in two by a Sawmill"... CURED with one bottle!

TULSA, OKLAHOMA: "Jammed to jelly in a Linseed Mill" ... CURED with one bottle!

... But here comes the greatest cure of them all from a Banker's Clerk in NEW YORK CITY. I shall read direct from his letter,—quote, and unquote: "While venturing too close to a powder factory at Farnsworth, New York, I was by a sudden explosion blown to a million atoms! By this unfortunate accident, I was rendered unfit for business.... About this time, I heard of your Wonderful, Grand Eliptical, Ecclesiastical, Pan-acure-all, and was persuaded to make use thereof. The first bottle gathered together my scattered particles. The second bottle animated my shattered frame. The third bottle was a complete cure! ... And the fourth bottle sent me back to Wall Street to count out money, make out bills-of-exchange, and render an account of that Wonderful, Grand Eliptical, Ecclesi-astical Panacure-all or Nervous Cordial that cures ALL dis-orders incidental to humanity!"

ONLY ONE DOLLAR A BOTTLE—SIX BOTTLES FOR FIVE DOLLARS!—WHO'LL BE THE NEXT CURE?— WHO'LL BE THE NEXT?"

... And—believe it or not—within one minute I saw thirty people push their way up to that stand, and jam that faker's brown derby full to the brim with dollar notes!

You'll go to your grave, wondering whether I was one of the thirty....

Now I know what you are thinking. You are saying to yourself, "Why has Frank told that story?"

Well, I'll tell you why I've told it: I hung around that stand until everyone else had moved on. Then I said to this fellow: "Would you mind if I ask you a few questions?"

"Nah ... go right ahead."

"Were you always this way?"

"Whatta yuh mean was I always this way?"

"Did you always have this terrific enthusiasm? Were you born this way?"

"Nah ..." he grinned. "Listen, when I first started to sell this stuff, I wasn't even makin' expenses. Then one day, I noticed when I put some punch into my talk, people began to buy. And even to this day, after all these years, I notice my sales go up and down, according to the amount of enthusiasm I put into my sales talk."

Just think: if false enthusiasm, *false* enthusiasm, can do that for a rank faker, selling a fake patent-medicine ... imagine what real, honest-to-goodness enthusiasm can do when you are trying sincerely to HELP people.

You know, the word enthusiasm comes from the ancient Greek—meaning *God within You!* Miller Huggins said something profound when he said, "If you will apply this ingredient to every one of those thirteen principles, you can become one of the greatest life insurance men in America!"

How do you become enthusiastic? There is just one simple rule: To Become enthusiastic, ACT enthusiastic!

Wouldn't you like to put that rule to the test right now?

Stand up where you are this minute, and give the "Christy Mathewson windup," repeating these words with all the enthusiasm you can generate:

> FORCE YOURSELF TO ACT
> ENTHUSIASTIC — and you'll
> *BECOME* ENTHUSIASTIC!

· · · · · · ·

... Apply this magic ingredient to every one of these principles during the next thirteen weeks, and be prepared to see astonishing results. It may easily revolutionize your entire life!

Make a high and holy resolve that you will double the amount of enthusiasm that you have been putting into your work and into your life!... If you carry out that resolve, and apply this ingredient to every one of the thirteen principles during the next thirteen weeks, be prepared to see astonishing results. It will probably double your income, and double your happiness.

How do you begin? There is just one rule: To become enthusiastic, *act* enthusiastic!

> "If you can give your son or daughter only one
> gift, let it be Enthusiasm!"
> ... BRUCE BARTON

Chapter 15

THE LEFT-HANDED, CROSS-EYED, KNOCK-KNEED PITCHER FROM NEW ORLEANS!

AT THE FIDELITY'S REGIONAL MEETING in New Orleans, the first thing I showed them was the telegram I had just received from Miller Huggins about the New York Yankees "agreeing to *double* their enthusiasm during the balance of the season." This seemed to fire up our sessions so much, we started all the meetings around the country the same way—with Huggins' wire!

Then I told them the story about the first time I ever set foot in that wonderful Old-World city of New Orleans. It was during a Spring training trip when I was with the St. Louis Cardinals. We stopped off to play a game with the Pelicans...

Pitching for New Orleans that day was a six-foot four awkward-looking, left-handed, cross-eyed, knock-kneed pitcher! All the players said he positively had the most deceptive delivery of any pitcher in baseball.

In the first inning, with one out, we got a man on first base and Roger Bresnahan, our manager, flashed the hit-and-run signal. The runner took a long lead off first base ready to go on the pitch, and the batter got set to "hit with the runner." It is one of the prettiest plays in baseball—when it works. But as that left-handed, cross-eyed, knock-kneed pitcher got ready to pitch, he had one eye on the batter, his other eye on the runner, and it was impossible to tell who he really was looking at!

Suddenly, he gave a strange jerk of his shoulder, lifted his right knee almost up to his chin and his body swung around as though he was throwing the ball over to first base. The runner dove back into the bag, while the batter stood watching this play down at first base. But by a freak twist of his body, that pitcher shot the ball with amazing speed right over the heart of the plate.

"STRIKE ONE!" roared the umpire.

"Come on, wake up out here!" shouted Bresnahan, and again he gave the hit-and-run signal.

The runner pulled his cap down tighter, edging his way carefully off first base, ready to get going with the next pitch. Again that left-handed, cross-eyed, knock-kneed pitcher had one eye on the runner, the other eye on the batter, gave this strange jerk of the shoulder, lifted his knee, turning his back almost to the batter. This time it looked as though he just had to throw the ball to first base. Back the runner lunged, head first into the bag, and the batter stood flat-footed watching the play at first base. But to the batter's amazement, a curve ball shot by him right over the plate before he could get his bat up.

"STRIKE T-W-O!" bellowed the umpire.

"What the hell's the matter with you pin-headed idiots?" screamed Bresnahan. *"Keep yer eyes open!"*

Unfortunately, from his location over on the third-base coaching line, it was impossible for Bresnahan to see what was causing this confusion. So again, he flashed the hit-and-run signal, a rare thing to do with two strikes on the batter.

The runner took a bigger lead off first, and the batter dug a deeper toe-hold. It was plain to see they weren't to be fooled the third time.

Once more, that loose-jointed, left-handed, cross-eyed pitcher lifted his knee and twisted his body around—off dashed the runner on his way to second; and the batter started swinging. Only *this* time the pitcher *did* throw the ball to first base—but the big muscled batter couldn't stop swinging!

The catcher pounded his fist in his big glove so hard it sounded just like the ball.

"STRIKE THREE YER OUT!" roared the umpire, swinging one hand high over his head.

Imagine the astonished expression on the runner's face when he arrived at second base and saw the second baseman standing there waiting for him *with the ball.*

"YER OUT!" screamed the base umpire, completing one of the most amazing double plays in baseball.

... Now this play would have been the last one I'd expect could help me later in life. But after I got into selling, I made a surprising discovery. Many people I interviewed reminded me of that left-handed, cross-eyed, knock-kneed pitcher from New Orleans. By keeping records, I found that two out of three times, people—either intentionally or unintentionally—gave me the wrong pitch. Two out of three times they gave me the wrong target to shoot at!

Showing these records one time to Billy Walker, a master salesman, he said smiling, "I know just what you mean. I went all through that myself."

"How did you ever overcome this problem, Mr. Walker?" I asked.

He then told me something I've never forgotten: "Frank, you never know what's in a man's mind by what he says. When a man offers objections, he doesn't mean he won't buy. What he really means is that you haven't convinced him yet. You haven't produced enough evidence to make him want to buy!"

... Remembering that *deceptive delivery* of the left-handed, cross-eyed, knock-kneed pitcher from New Orleans,—and Billy Walker's basic rule: "Produce enough evidence to make him *want* to buy"—made the difference between my being "anchored on first base," and making a sale by *"touching all the bases!"*

I also found it equally important to remember in dealing with *everyone*, in everyday living—even with my own children.

Chapter 16

CHRISTY MATHEWSON'S BULLS-EYE

Looking back across the years, I am astounded how many of the principles I first learned in baseball I was able to apply later on in business and everyday living. For example, shortly after I joined the St. Louis Cardinals, Jack Bliss, our third string catcher, broke his leg. That left the Cardinals with only two catchers. So, for a few weeks, I found myself down in the bullpen warming up pitchers.

I didn't like this at all, because I wasn't a catcher, and thought I wasn't learning anything down there. But all the time I was learning a lesson that years later became priceless to me.

The best pitcher for the Cardinals at that time was "Slim Sallee." I can still hear "Sal" yell: "Frank, hold yer glove up!" He never would pitch the ball until I held the big catcher's glove up for his target; and he made me shift the target for each pitch. The "pocket" in the center of the glove was the "Bull's-Eye."

Sallee was the only pitcher on the team who made me give him a target. And he was the only pitcher on the team who had good control. Sal studied the weakness of batters and, when he got out on the mound in the game, he knew exactly where he wanted to pitch to each batter—and he seldom failed to put the ball there!

One time I asked Sal where he got this idea. He said: "From the greatest pitcher in baseball, Christy Mathewson."

Just before the game one day at the Polo Grounds in New York, I told Mathewson what Sallee had said and asked Matty about it. I never forgot the great pitcher's answer. He said: "Throwing a ball without a target, is like shooting a gun off into the air. *No gunner ever becomes a sharpshooter without aiming at the bull's-eye!*"

Not long after Billy Walker taught me to "hang on longer and produce enough evidence," I got one of the biggest thrills of my life! I was able to close a sale so large that it created somewhat of a sensation in our company. I was astounded when they announced that it was one of the largest individual sales ever made in their history.

Since it was made by a green dub like me, who had never finished grade school, it aroused a widespread curiosity. A few weeks later I was invited to tell my story at a convention in Boston.

But I was shocked when one of the country's foremost salesmen, Clayton M. Hunsicker, came up to me following my talk, congratulated me, then said: "I still doubt whether you understand exactly *why* you were able to make that sale."

I asked him what he meant.

He then told me something I soon learned was the most profound secret of dealing with people.

What he told me that day, among other things, was that *every living person wants something.* Our job was to find out what people wanted, then help them find the best way to get it. "That's the bull's-eye of selling anything! In the first minute of your interview with that man, you took a blind stab and accidentally stumbled onto what he wanted. Then you kept him talking more about it, asking more questions about it, never letting him get away from the thing he wanted. Then you showed him how to get it!"

Later that day, I told Mr. Hunsicker the story about Slim Sallee yelling at me down in the bullpen—and what Christy Mathewson had said about always aiming at the bull's eye!

"That's a wonderful example... *now you've got it!*" he declared. "It's the same principle. Most salesmen are like those pitchers who wind up and throw the ball, not knowing or even trying to find out what the target is. If you will always remember this one rule, and practice it every day like Christy Mathewson did, selling, and dealing with people in all walks of life will be easy!"

Do you know something? I believe it is just possible that I might eventually have gone back to collecting on a bicycle if Clayton Hunsicker hadn't taught me this profound principle. At the time, I thought he had discovered a new idea. But I soon learned that another man right here in my home town of Philadelphia had the same idea 180 years before I met Mr. Hunsicker. Let me give you one example of how he applied it. Let's watch how *he* "hit the Bull's-Eye":

This man had invented a new kind of stove. He realized that it must be *sold.* So he wrote his own advertisement. He directed his sales pitch to *others,*—more specifically—to *women!* Here it is:

> Because of poor heating systems, women get colds in the head, rheums, and defluxions, which fall into their jaws and gums, and have destroyed many a fine set of teeth in these northern colonies. Great and bright fires do very much contribute to damage the eyes, dry and shrival the skin, and bring an early appearance of old age.

Did this idea sell? You've already guessed the answer. Is it any wonder that his stove quickly became a best-seller throughout all the Colonies? Governor Thomas of Pennsylvania was so pleased with the construction that he offered to give Franklin a patent for the sole vending of them. But Franklin declined it from a principle that ". . . as we enjoy great advantages from the inventions of others, we should be glad of an opportunity to serve others by an invention of ours; and this we should do freely and generously."

The air-conditioning method of the famous Franklin stove is used as the basic principle in our present day modern airconditioners. Although Franklin finally had 105 inventions to his credit he never took out a patent!

This principle may sound queer, but later in life after Franklin had become rich, he wrote: "I found early that when I worked for myself alone, myself alone worked for me; but when I worked for others, others worked for me."

Soon after I began using this principle successfully in business—as taught me by Clayton Hunsicker—I had an opportunity to test it in my private life. The members of the Wynnefield United Presbyterian Church were conducting an all-community canvassing campaign to raise money for the building of a new Church and Bible School. We had outgrown our little stucco chapel. Two nights each week, for three weeks, all the workers met in the chapel and reported results of our canvassing.

One night, a worker told about an unpleasant experience he had encountered with a wealthy man he called on. "I've been a salesman all my life and have run into some pretty tough customers," said he, "but I never had anyone give me the rude, cold, brush-off he gave me!"

Our Building Fund Chairman admitted he had hesitated to

put Mr. "X" 's name on the list in the first place. About a year previously, this man had cut himself off from his community and church. His only son, a very fine young man of thirty-two, had been mysteriously and brutally murdered!

The father vowed he would spend the rest of his life if necessary to find the murderer. As time went on, without the crime being solved, this lonely, bitter man shut himself off from the world.

Everyone agreed it was a foolish waste of time to canvass him. They "gave him up"—not just as a contributor, but as a person. You could tell from the way they spoke about him, this man had chosen to be almost invisible in his community. Life would go on around him, but never in contact with him.

The Chairman was about to tear up the card and drop it in the waste-basket when I spoke up. "May I have that card? I've got an idea."

"Sure you may," laughed the Chairman, winking at the other men.

About eight-thirty the following evening, I rang the front doorbell of this man's large and beautiful home. It was in total darkness except for one small light on the first floor. After waiting a few minutes, I was about to leave when the door opened quietly, about six inches. It was Mr. X himself! The light from the lamp inside gave me a dim view of him. I thought I'd never seen a sadder face. "What did you want?" he asked.

"I'm a neighbor of yours, Mr. X. May I come in and talk with you a few minutes?"

"*What about?*" he demanded, eyeing me suspiciously. I could feel the intense hatred in his voice.

"About your son," was all I said.

I waited quietly, but looked him straight in the eye. It

seemed like a full minute before he spoke again. Finally, he said, "Come in."

He took me into a small study where the lamp was lighted; he was watching me closely every moment. "Sit down," he motioned.

"Mr. X," I spoke in a soft voice and with much feeling, "I know about the great loss you have had. I can feel for you with all my heart, because I have a son myself. Knowing how you feel, I thought as a memorial for your son, you might like to dedicate a beautiful stained-glass window in the new Church."

"How much would such a window cost?" he asked with interest.

"I really don't know," I admitted. "That would depend entirely on whatever you felt would be appropriate."

I was amazed how quickly he responded to the idea, after I listened to him talk out some of his unhappiness. In a very few minutes, I left there with his check for Five Thousand Dollars. When he handed me the check, he was too emotional to speak. And so was I.

The following evening, when the workers met in the little chapel, I handed our Chairman Mr. X's card and said, "You can put this back in the files now."

He looked at the card and saw scrawled across the face of it in my handwriting: Amount Pledged—$5,000.00. Laughing, as though he thought I was only trying to be funny, he asked: "Did you *really* go to see him?"

"Here's his check," I replied, passing it over without a smile.

The Chairman was speechless. He then passed the check around for everyone to see. Everybody was plainly astounded, and wanted to know what had happened!

"Well, frankly," I said, "my purpose in seeing Mr. X was not so much to get a large contribution, but to do something that would get him in touch with life again. My only hope was to say something that would touch the one tender spot in his heart . . . so I talked about a memorial for his beloved son."

Actually, all I had done was to apply the philosophy I had learned such a short while before: *Talk about what a man wants, and show him how to get it.*

What happened to this lonely man? Mr. X's act of dedicating the beautiful memorial for his son seemed to be just what he needed to get rid of the bitter hate which was eating his heart out. A stained-glass window led him out of the darkness, back to his friends, his business—to the world of doing, thinking, and living for others.

Remember what Christy Mathewson said: "Throwing a ball without a target is like shooting a gun off into the air. *No gunner ever became a sharpshooter without aiming at the Bulls-Eye!*"

Applied to everyday living: *Find out what the other person wants, then help him find the best way to get it.* . . The ancients first said it. It's *The Golden Rule in action!*

> ". . . accept my kind offices to Thy other children as the only return in my power for Thy continual favors to me." (*Closing words of Franklin's daily prayer.*)

Chapter 17

HOW HE CHANGED THE THINKING
OF THE WORLD!

About this time, I had been studying a book written by a prominent college professor on the *art of overcoming objections*. His stock answers to objections seemed so clever, I began committing them to memory. As soon as a man offered an objection, I would fire these smart answers back at him! That professor had never sold anything. Using his method, I wasn't selling anything either. It merely got me into arguments.

It was lucky for me that I stopped studying this book and started reading about a man who lived in Athens, Greece, twenty-three centuries ago. His name was Socrates. He accomplished something that few men in all history have been able to do—he changed the thinking of the world! Socrates was a teacher, a strange kind of teacher. His method was to *ask questions*; instead of telling people they were wrong. Frequently, the other person found he couldn't prove the truth of the things he had believed; his answers to Socrates' questions failed to fit some of his other answers. Thus, by a series of thoughtfully directed questions, Socrates would help the other person find out the truth for *himself*!

I might never have learned about the Socratic method if Franklin hadn't written about the effect it had on his life. As a struggling young businessman, Ben had trouble getting along with people. He was a tremendous worker, up every morning before dawn, working long hours. But he made enemies! One day, he was shocked when a Quaker friend told him that people were crossing on the other side of the street to avoid him! Studying the method of Socrates, Ben saw the wisdom of dropping his habit of abrupt contradiction, arguing, and making so many positive assertions.

"I began," he said, "putting on the *humble inquirer*, and I soon found the advantage of this change in my manner."

Ben took great delight in developing the question method, asking people questions on which he knew they could both agree. He said at first, he had to guard against a natural belligerent attitude—his *manner* of questioning implied that *he knew* he was right, and the other person absolutely wrong!

Ben found that he had to show he understood and respected the other person's point of view—even if he didn't agree with it.

He wrote: "I had less mortification when I was found to be in the wrong, and I more easily prevailed with others to give up their mistakes and join with me when I happened to be in the right ..."

Later, in an editorial, "Apology for Printers," June 10, 1731, he clearly stated his attitude when he said that people's opinions varied and that it was the printer's business to print them. "Printers are," he wrote, "educated in the belief that when men differ in opinion, both sides ought equally to have the advantage of being heard by the public; and that *when truth and error have fair play, the former is always an overmatch for the latter."*

Ben became expert at drawing out truths. Many years later the Colonies sent him to England to see if he could negotiate an agreement on the heavy taxes being imposed. He appeared before the House of Commons. His conduct and replies to members of the House in ten days of cross-examination prompted Edmund Burke, the great English statesman and member of Parliament, to compare Franklin to a master being quizzed by a group of schoolboys!

I resolved that from then on, I would make it a major ambition of mine to cultivate this great art which he mastered to such a high degree—*The Socratic Method.* I made a bet with members of my family to pay ten cents every time anyone caught me saying *anything* if I failed to put it in the form of a question. At the end of one week, I called off the bet. I had filled a piggy-bank full of dimes. I found myself shaking dimes out of the piggy-bank for carfare! But this little game was lots of fun for the family and really helped me get started right— quicker. In addition, it had a double-barreled effect. It had all of us in the house "thinking twice . . . before speaking once."

. . . One Sunday morning, I was walking home from church with my son, Lyle. I had started teaching a class of boys in the Bible School. Lyle was in the class. With so little previous knowledge of the Bible at that time, I found trying to hold the attention of those boys about the toughest job I ever tackled. But that Sunday, I thought I did pretty well. I waited for Lyle to compliment me. But not a word. Finally, I said, "Well, Lyle, what did you think of the lesson I taught this morning?" Lyle hesitated, then said: "Dad, I'm sorry, but I wasn't listening to you very much; my mind was on something else." This surprised me, because he had looked at me all through the lesson.

Now I began the Question Method of teaching. The boys became much more interested, actually excited about the lesson. *They* were *participating!* What was even more important, weeks later, by questioning them, I found they *remembered* much more.

One morning, the minister asked me if I would give a five minute review of the lesson from the platform. All I did was ask questions. I was astonished by the enthusiastic response from both young and old. That was the shortest five minutes I can ever remember. For several Sundays afterward, the minister had me give a five minute review. I asked questions, *and had them tell me!*

Next thing I knew . . . I was elected Superintendent!

Would you believe it? A little *one-word question* had something to do with winning World War II. Sounds fantastic, doesn't it? It happened like this:

During the War, the United States War Department was trying to find some company which could produce an emergency food for our boys fighting in the torrid zone. It had to be small enough to carry in their pockets, yet contain sufficient nourishment to tide over a starving flier, soldier, or marine; and at the same time, keep him immune from tropical fever!

The Quartermaster's Department consulted with companies all over the country, but the answer was always the same: "It couldn't be done!"

They were about ready to give up the idea, when someone suggested seeing this young fellow, Milton Hershey, up in Hershey, Pennsylvania. Hershey was only eighty-five years old!

"*Why?*" asked Mr. Hershey. "*Why* can't it be done?"

"Because nothing will stand up in that tropical climate," they told him.

"Why not?" persisted Hershey. And he kept asking "Why?" until he had all the problems clear, and all the reasons why "it couldn't be done."

Over cigars, around his table, he said: "It will take some time to study these facts. But we've got the problem clear. Now, one of us has got to find the answer."

Experiments began at the Hershey plant. Working three shifts, day and night, they soon shipped 75,000 Chocolate Bars to the South Pacific. Each bar contained 150 units of Vitamin B-1 to prevent tropic diseases; also 600 calories of nourishment. These chocolate bars performed the "impossible." Soon huge shipments of these new secret weapons were being sent to our boys all over the world.

An amazing story? Yes. However, there is an earlier part of the "Milton Hershey Story" which is equally amazing, and even more inspiring to me: Hershey had experienced failure after failure until he was forty years old. At forty, he found himself pushing a candy pushcart around the streets. One day one of the wheels came off and his candy was dumped all over the street. People passing by picked up pieces and walked off eating them. Hershey was so discouraged, he sat down on the curb and buried his head in his hands. "*Why?*" he asked himself, "why is it that other men succeed and I fail?" Putting himself through a long quiz, he narrowed the answer down to one reason: "*I was going ahead without having all the facts!*"

From that day, until his death—forty-eight years later—Milton Hershey dedicated his whole life to the philosophy of asking "*Why?...Why not?*" This, he believed, kept him alert and young in mind. And it helped make him a fortune of many millions. Asking "Why?" or "Why not?" he became known as the original "Doctor Quiz."

Well, basically, isn't the whole philosophy of Socrates built around that simple little question: "Why?" ... Why not?"

Chapter 18

AN ALGEBRAIC METHOD FOR MAKING
A DECISION

O NE GEM OF AN IDEA which has helped me all through life whenever a complex problem arose that had me worried, and needed clarifying, I got from Old Ben. Here it is, in Ben's own words—words that should be inscribed on a bronze plaque and hung in every home and school, every shop and office:

WHY?   WHY NOT?

> In the affairs of so much importance to you, wherein you ask my advice, I cannot for want of sufficient premises, advise you *what* to determine, but if you please I will tell you *how*.
> When these difficult cases occur, they are difficult chiefly because while we have them under consideration all the reasons *pro* and *con* are not present to the mind at the same time; but sometimes one set present themselves, and at other times another, the first being out of sight. Hence, the various purposes or inclinations that alternately prevail, and the uncertainty that perplexes us ...

To get over this, my way is, to divide half a sheet of paper by a line into two columns, writing over the one *PRO*, and over the other *CON*. Then during three or four days consideration, I put down under the different heads short hints of the different motives that at different times occur to me *for* or *against* the measure.

When I have thus got them all together in one view, I endeavor to estimate their respective weights; and where I find two (one on each side) that seem equal, I strike them both out. If I find a reason *pro* equal to some *two* reasons *con*, I strike out the *three*. If I judge some *two* reasons *con* equal to some *three* reasons *pro*, I strike out the *five*; and thus proceeding I find at length where the *balance* lies; and if, after a day or two of further consideration nothing new that is of importance occurs on either side, I come to a determination accordingly. And tho' the weight of reasons cannot be taken with the precision of algebraic quantities, yet, when each is thus considered separately and comparatively, and the whole lies before me, I think I can judge better, and am less likely to take a rash step; and in fact I have found great advantage from this kind of equation in what may be called *Moral* or *Prudential Algebra* ... Wishing sincerely that you may determine for the best, I am ever, my dear friend,

Yours most affectionately,
B. Franklin

In selling, one of the toughest objections I encountered was: "I haven't made up my mind whether I'm going to take it or not."

I say, "My job is to help you in making up your mind. You don't have to think over . . . ." Then I draw a line down the middle of a sheet of paper and sum it all up with *Questions—* Why? on one side and Why not? on the other—the "Algebraic

Method!" This helps people crystallize their thinking. Their answers usually add up to what they *really* want. They like it this way. It's *their own* decision!

Imitate Socrates. Questions, rather than positive assertions are the most effective way to find out what people want or need ... *Inquire* rather than *attack*.

Show that you respect the other person's point of view.

> "*When truth and error have fair play, the former is always an overmatch for the latter*" ... Franklin

One of the biggest things you get out of a college education is a questioning attitude, a habit of demanding and weighing evidence ... a scientific approach.

If you have a decision to make of great importance—try the Algebraic Method:

Why?	*Why Not?*

Chapter 19

PUT STOPPERS ON CHOPPERS FOR SUCCESS

THE LATE CHARLES STEINMETZ, electrical genius of the General Electric Company said, "No man becomes a fool until he stops asking questions." Well, I became a fool *after* I began asking questions—because I stopped *listening!*

First: my problem was I was afraid to talk; second: after taking the Public Speaking Course, and serving as a Four-Minute-Man, I found that I *loved* to talk. In fact, I became so proficient at talking, I forgot all about *listening!*

One day, one of my best friends took me aside and kindly told me about this unpardonable fault of mine. Referring to another well known ear-pounder—who he tactfully assured me was much worse than I—he said, "I actually walk five blocks out of my way to avoid him and still *save time!*"

Only a few days later I met another friend I hadn't seen for some time. He spoke cordially enough but definitely avoided me. In fact, I thought he looked as though he was ready to *run* if I approached him. Then I remembered that the last time we met I gave his ear an awful pounding. Do you know something?—I don't think people ever get over that. They are never quite the same again.

Ben Franklin found listening so important, he wrote: "My desire to gain knowledge, and considering that in conversation it was obtained rather by the use of the ears than of the tongue, and therefore wishing to break a bad habit I was getting into, which only made me acceptable to trifling company, I gave *Silence* the *second place*."

Years later Franklin became known as the "World's greatest diplomat." Listen to these words he wrote; anyone might profit by reading them from time to time:

"The Wit of Conversation consists more in finding it in others, than showing a great deal yourself. He who goes out of your company pleased with his own Facetiousness and Ingenuity, will the sooner come into it again. Most men had rather *please* than admire you, and seek less to be instructed and diverted, than approved and applauded, and it is certainly the most delicate sort of Pleasure, to please another."

Ed Murrow, famous for his "Person to Person" interviews on Television, was asked how he managed to draw people out to talk so interestingly. He replied, "I merely try to direct conversation by injecting a question at the strategic moment, then *listen*. Somehow the pressure to avoid dead air is on the subject. He often gives you his best stuff after a short period of silence, *if you wait him out*."

Here's a little three-point formula that became a life-saver for me. Here it is in capsule form:

1. Find out what the other person is interested in.

2. Try to direct his conversation with questions he will enjoy answering.

3. Then, *LISTEN!* Nothing else is so flattering as that.

A few years ago I wrote an article on "Listening." The title was "The Forgotten Art That is Magic in Selling," and was syndicated in a number of newspapers. One mid-western paper gave it a new title. They called it: *"Put Stoppers on Choppers for Success."* I liked it so much that I adopted it for this chapter.

I was up in Maine on a fishing vacation one summer with Dale Carnegie. One rainy day there wasn't much we could do but talk. I asked Dale how he happened to get started in this business of leadership training and effective speaking. I already knew most of the story but had never heard it in full. Besides I thought Dale would like to hear it again himself anyhow! It really was an exciting story. When he finished, I began asking him some more questions such as, "What are your plans for the next ten years?" etc. Finally, our fishing guide called us for lunch. Surprised, Dale looked at his watch and said, "Frank, do you realize what you've done? You've been listening to me for *three hours!*"

Two years later Dale called me on the phone from Memphis, Tennessee, and prevailed on me to fly down there and join him on a lecture tour. He said, "Frank, I know you can do this work and you'll *love* it . . . . Besides, I like to be with you."

That was the beginning of a two year tour that I will tell you more about later. Come to think of it, I probably would never have written this book or any other book if I hadn't made those lecture tours; and I would never have gone on the road with Dale if I hadn't adopted that little three point formula!

Dr. Norman Vincent Peale recently wrote: "Many people who complain that their prayers are not effective, fail to remember that *listening* is just as much a part of prayer as *talking!*"

Much of the three years of Jesus's ministry was spent *listen-*

ing to the troubles of others. Often, when He needed counsel and guidance Himself, He went off into the hills all alone for long periods of meditation to—*listen to His Father!*

Show the other person that you are sincerely interested in what he is saying; give him all the eager attention and appreciation that he craves and is so hungry for, but seldom gets. *Listen* with *enthusiasm!*

If you would be a good conversationalist, remember: "The wit of conversation consists more in finding it in Others, than showing a great deal yourself."

A MAGIC three-point formula:

1. Find out what the other person is interested in.
2. Try to direct his conversation with questions he will enjoy answering.
3. Then, *LISTEN!*

PRAYER
For This Week

"O God, lift me out of the rush and the turmoil of life, that I may find the strength that comes from fellowship with Thee. Give me a quiet mind, a teachable heart and a willingness to wait on Thy guidance and direction. May I learn how to listen as well as to speak, and in the stillness may I hear Thy voice. Refresh me in the quiet hour for the responsibilities of the day . . . through Jesus Christ. *Amen.*"

—Alfred Grant Walton, Brooklyn, N. Y.
Minister, Flatbush-Tompkins Congregational Church

Chapter 20

RESOLUTION

Hᴉsᴛᴏʀʏ ᴛᴇʟʟs ᴜs that making New Year's resolutions is the number one ancient custom. According to nation-wide polls, however, few of us keep our resolutions beyond the first few days or weeks.

Why? Science now tells us we have been going about it the wrong way; but if we follow the simple method conceived by one of the world's greatest scientists, we will find that, instead of a "straightjacket," it can be a lot of fun with rich rewards.

Conquering *himself* was one of young Franklin's greatest problems. Years later, he became a scientist and had 105 inventions to his credit, yet this simple, though scientific method on how to keep resolutions has never been counted as one of his inventions. But, judging from the amazing response to the *International* event in 1956—celebrating the 250th Anniversary of Franklin's birth—this idea may soon become more useful than *all of his 105 inventions combined!*

In Franklin's eightieth year, he attributed his remarkable health, and *all his success and happiness*, to following the *thirteen weeks' method*. He wrote: "Though my plan was not wholly without religion, there was in it no mark of any of the distinguishing tenets of any particular sect. I had purposely avoided them; for being fully persuaded of the utility and excellency of my method, and that it might be serviceable to people in all religions, I would not have anything in it that should prejudice any one, of any sect, against it ... Intending some time to publish it, I purposed writing a comment on virtue, in which I would have shown the advantages of possessing it, and the mischiefs attending its opposite vice; and I should have called my book *The Art of Virtue*, because it would have shown the means and manner of obtaining virtue, which would have distinguished it from the mere exhortation to be good, that does not instruct and indicate the means, but is like the apostle's man of verbal charity, who only without showing it to the naked and hungry how or where they might get clothes or victuals, exhorted them to be fed and clothed.—James ii. 15, 16."

"Vicious actions are not hurtful because they are forbidden, but forbidden because they are hurtful, the nature of man alone considered; that it was, therefore, every one's interest to be virtuous who wished to be happy even in this world ... "

Extremely human and practical, however, Franklin wrote: " ... any man who exacted perfection of himself—if it became known—would make himself ridiculous ... "

It seemed to Ben, that, if God expected us to be perfect, He would have made us perfect—or made it possible for us to achieve the heights of perfection ... "So, a benevolent man should allow a few faults in himself, to keep his friends in countenance."

"In truth," wrote Ben, "I found myself incorrigible with respect to *Order*. This Principle cost me so much painful attention, and my faults in it vexed me so much, and I had such frequent relapses, that I was almost ready to give up the attempt, and content myself with a faulty character in that respect, like the man who, in buying an ax of a smith, my neighbor, desired to have the whole surface as bright as the edge. The smith consented to grind it bright for him if he would turn the wheel; he turned, while the smith pressed the broad face of the ax hard and heavily on the stone, which made the turning very fatiguing. The man came every now and then from the wheel to see how the work went on, and at length would take his ax as it was, without further grinding.

"'No,' said the smith, 'turn on, turn on; we shall have it bright by-and-by; as yet, it is only speckled.'

"'Yes,' says the man, 'but I think I liked a speckled ax best.'"

So, when young Ben proceeded with his thirteen weeks' idea —giving a week's strict attention to each of the virtues successively—he found this simple plan a truly *magic formula*. He wrote: "And like him who, having a garden to weed, does not attempt to eradicate all the bad herbs at once, which would exceed his reach and strength, but works on *one* of the beds at a time, and, having accomplished the first, proceeds to the *second*, so I had the encouraging pleasure of seeing on my pages the progress I made...."

Chapter 21

"I'VE GOT A WHOLE TRUNK FULL OF 'EM"

I WAS PASSING THROUGH Johnstown, Pennsylvania, on a train recently, and a strange thrill went all through me as I looked out the Pullman window. We were moving along slowly at about ten miles an hour, when suddenly there was the old ball-park, Point Stadium—the same grounds I played on more than half a century ago. It sets on that point of ground right at the junction of Stony Creek and Little Conemaugh, which form the big Conemaugh River.

Memories began racing through my head just as vivid and clear as if they had happened only last week. I could see the faces, hear the voices, even some of the exact words of many of the players on the team: "Humpty" Badel, a homely little hunchback, but one of the most sensational ballplayers I ever saw perform; a natural left-handed hitter, terrific baserunner!— next to Ty Cobb, the players said, the most amazing slider into bases they ever saw! "Humpty" would have been one of the truly great big-league outfielders if he had lived. But during the season he became seriously ill, and died shortly afterward of tuberculosis. . . .

I could see Kooperman, our catcher with a marvelous throwing arm. "Koop" was one of the survivors of the Johnstown Flood ... "Chappie" Chapelle, the huge, handsome blonde pitcher, who loved "life" too much—or he might have been another Christy Mathewson. I could hear Chappie under the shower after he'd pitched a winning game, shouting to the top of his lungs, *"Hold 'er"* ... *"Hold 'er."* I never did find out what he meant by "Hold 'er!"

... Then I heard Bert Conn, our manager, say to me: "Frank, I fired you because you're *lazy!*" I heard his voice loud and clear, right there in the Pullman—half a century later.

And then, I remembered, what to me, was the most unforgettable character of all. His name was Denny Wolf. I had never met Denny before, but I remembered seeing him pitch for the Phillies a few years earlier. He was red hot then, had the makings of one of the great pitchers of baseball. I always wondered why the Phillies let him get away from them. I found out *why* in Johnstown. Denny had an enemy. He was an alcoholic.

They put him in to pitch one day. Word passed around among the players: "This is Denny's last chance." Everybody tried extra hard, because we liked Denny and wanted to help him. But the breaks went bad for him, and the manager let him stay in to "take his beating." The dramatic end came in the eighth inning. When the score was 11-2, Denny went up to bat and hit a terrific home run that disappeared over the left-center field fence.

The crowd gave him a rather weak and polite applause. As Denny arrived back to our bench, he pulled out a piece of paper from his hip pocket, tore it up into pieces, and threw it at the manager as he said bitterly: "Here, you know whatcha kin do with that ... *I've got a whole trunkful of 'em!*"

That paper was Denny's unconditional release, handed to

him, I learned afterward, just before he went up to bat and hit
that home run.

Two days later, somebody said to me, "Say, Frank, you're
from Philadelphia, aren't you?"

"Yes," I nodded.

"Well, there's a Philadelphia pal of yours down at Tony's.
He's in a bad way. I think you'd better go down and help him."

When I arrived at Tony's, I found it was a dirty barroom.
There was Denny Wolf, dead drunk, and dead broke. After
he'd spent all his pay-off money, Tony tried to throw him out,
but hadn't quite made the grade with Denny, drunk as he was.

Denny's suitcase was under a table in the corner. I picked
it up, half-lifted Denny's dead weight and said, "Come on
Denny, let's go."

He looked up at me, and, to my surprise, recognized me.
"We're going home, Denny," I said quietly.

The "Pennsy" Station was only a block away. Denny managed to walk along, but as we approached the station he
stopped suddenly. "I'm broke," he announced. I handed him
enough money to pay for his ticket home and said, "Here's a
little extra, Denny. Get yourself something to eat on the train,
and you'll feel better."

Denny cried. It was a drunk's cry, but he really seemed
grateful.

Three days later, someone said: "I thought you told us Denny
Wolf went home."

"So he did," I replied, "I saw him get on the train for Philadelphia."

"Well, he's down at Tony's, drunker than ever. And Tony
says if somebody don't take 'im away soon he's gonna break
his head!"

This time, I bought his ticket myself, took him to his seat

on the train, handed him one dollar and gave the ticket to the conductor, who promised to keep an eye on Denny. I hoped I'd never see him again in my life.

A year later, early one Sunday morning, I stepped off the train in Hazleton, Pennsylvania. I was playing at the time for Hazleton in the Atlantic League. The defunct Colonial League had closed on July 4th, and I was glad to get a job of any kind. Hazleton, that morning, seemed deserted. Not a living thing stirred, as a dreary looking bunch of bush-league ballplayers carried their suitcases up the street.

Suddenly I noticed a blackened face peeping around the corner across the street. As I took a double-take look, the face pulled back. I had a peculiar feeling that this person was watching *me*.

When we got up to the main street, I was able to get a full view of the man. He stood motionless against the red brick wall. He obviously was a tramp, his face black with coal dirt. As we all walked toward the old Valley Hotel, I turned and looked back. The tramp waved to me. I recognized him. It was Denny Wolf!

I wanted to see Denny about as much as you would want to see a tax-collector. But I knew I had no choice. I motioned for him to wait.

After I got my suitcase up to my room, I went down and met Denny. He was completely sober, swore he hadn't had a drink for six weeks and was "through with the poison forever!"

Somehow, I believed him. He looked so pitiful, my heart went out for him. I said: "What are you doing up here in Hazleton?"

"I read in the paper that you were playin' for Hazleton. I made up my mind I was gonna get up here somehow, so I freighted it up."

I said: "Denny, you were one of the best looking young pitchers in baseball only three years ago. How old are you now?"

"Only twenty-six."

"You're still young," I said, talking like a much older man. (I was only nineteen.) "We need another pitcher here, bad. If you are really through with drink, I'll get you straightened out and maybe this is just the chance you need to stage a comeback."

Denny said frankly, "I couldn't go in and pitch today, but if you could give me a week, *I'll show you the best pitcher in this league!*"

I smuggled him in the back way of the hotel, and up the back stairs to the room. My roommate, Jack Lapp, was unpacking. Jack was speechless when he saw the bum I'd brought in. I explained the situation in a hushed voice; briefly as I could . . . "and," I wound up, "within ten days Denny will show you the best pitching you ever caught. Within thirty days, you and Denny will go to the big leagues as a sensational battery!"

My prediction turned out to be fifty per cent correct.

The big leagues idea appealed to Jack. First thing, we got Denny to take a good tub bath. Then he shaved a two-weeks' growth of beard off his face. We dressed him up in some respectable clothes of ours. He had black hair, black eyes, and we were surprised what a good looking guy we took down to the dining room with us.

Denny was hungrier than a bear after a long winter's sleep.

Two days later, it was hard to believe this was the same man. We took him out to the ballgrounds and introduced him to Jim Brady, our manager. Denny told Jim he was through with drink forever. Jim got all excited and gave Denny a Hazleton uniform.

When Denny Wolf warmed up that day in front of a crowded

grandstand, he looked like "Spaulding's Guide!" He had the most beautiful wind-up and follow-through we'd ever seen. I thought he was overdoing it a bit, but, when he finished, the crowd applauded enthusiastically. Brady put him on the pay-roll starting that day.

We could hardly wait for him to pitch his first game. Each day, after he'd warm up, Brady would say, "How about it Denny, are you ready?"

"Not yet," was his reply, "give me another day or two."

After two weeks of this, one day in Wilkes-barre, Brady said, "Denny, you've got to go in there today. If you're not ready now, you'll never be."

It just happened that Sam Kennedy, Connie Mack's first full-time scout, manager of Baltimore in the defunct Union League, and former New Haven star first-baseman, was there looking for some "future greats." I told Sam to keep his eye on Hazleton's battery, Wolf and Lapp! That evening, after the game, Sam Kennedy signed up Jack Lapp—his "first find"—for Connie Mack's Athletics. Jack went to Philadelphia and quickly became a star catcher in the American League.

What happened to Denny Wolf? He proved that day that he was only a shell of the man he'd been. Every Wilkes-barre player took a toe-hold and swung for the fences. I never saw so many long drives in my life. We were afraid some of the infielders were going to get killed.

That night, four of us were eating quietly at a small table in the hotel dining room. Denny was one of the four. Freddie Weherle, a natural comedian with a decided Hoboken accent, had nothing to say . . . a rare thing for Fred. As he chewed slowly with a painful expression on his face, I said, "What's the matter with you, Freddie?"

"Sore tongue," he moaned.

"What have you got—a canker?"

"Nah. Me tongue is all *sunburnt*," declared Freddie.

"Sunburnt!" I exclaimed in astonishment.

"Yeah. Me tongue was hangin' out all afternoon chasin' dem terrific drives all over thuh outfield."

Denny exploded. "If you'd been playin' in the right position, yuh coulda caught every one of 'em in yer hip pocket!"

The following winter, during a driving snowstorm one night, our gang was walking home from a basketball game; and we passed "Billy-the-Bouncer's" Saloon on Ridge Avenue in Philadelphia. This Billy weighed three hundred pounds, and had become famous for throwing out more drunks than any other saloon-keeper in town.

Suddenly, we heard loud voices, then . . . Wham! something hit the wide swinging doors leading out of Billy's place and a drunk came flying through the air, landing in the deep snow out in the gutter. *You guessed it.* It was Denny Wolf. He didn't seem to be hurt as he got up, but he could just about navigate. We watched the poor guy 'til he got about thirty yards away, then one of our fellows yelled, "Yer all in, Denny!"

Denny reeled around and yelled back, "I kin lick anybody in thuh crowd!"

Nobody accepted the challenge. Finally, he spat and staggered on.

"Yer arm's gone, Denny!" shouted another guy, much louder.

Back came Denny. I pulled my cap down over my eyes and stood in the background. I didn't want Denny to see me.

"I kin lick any two of youse punks!" he declared.

Nobody said a word.

"So yuh think me arm's gone do yuh? . . . I kin throw a snowball farther than any of you smart dopes right now," challenged

9

Denny. Still not a word from anybody. "Yer YELLA! NO GUTS!" declared Denny with the greatest contempt. Off he started again.

After he got a safe distance away, one of the gang threw a hard snowball with all his might. He didn't intend to hit Denny, but it just missed his ear. "THE PRESIDENT WANTS TO SEE YOU, DENNY!" yelled big Bill Morrissey.

"TELL THE PRESIDENT TUH GO TUH HELL! I got a whole trunkfull of 'em." And Denny staggered on.

Chapter 22

"LICK HIM IN THE FIRST ROUND!"

On the night of September 27, 1930, it seemed as if every man, woman, and child in America was thrilled by blazing front-page headlines in all the newspapers throughout the nation: "ST. LOUIS CARDINALS CLINCH NATIONAL LEAGUE PENNANT!"

All the world loves the under dog who fights his way up from the bottom and reaches the top! That's what the Cardinals had done. They were twelve games behind in August, but they won twenty-one out of twenty-five games in September. On the way up, finally, everybody with any red blood in his veins was watching and talking about the Cardinals' astounding climb. Now they had made it!

But there was a *sensational story* behind this story, that had a double-barreled effect on me. Sixteen years before, when I was tumbling down the back steps of baseball, "Gabby" Street —then on the way down himself—did a "Good Samaritan" act for me at Chattanooga. A little, old mongrel dog had brought me back off the bridge. But it was "Gabby" who met me coming back into our hotel and noticed my blood-shot eyes.

"Gabby" not only convinced me that I wasn't licked, but out of his own pocket he sent telegrams to several of his friends around the country to get me another job. The *only* reason Galveston, Texas, took me on was because of their confidence in "Gabby" Street.

Now—sixteen years later—I'm reading front-page headlines about those amazing "Cards"—and "Gabby Street" is their manager!

Two days later, the New Champions came to Philadelphia to play the Phillies. Can you imagine anything stopping me from going out to see that game, and to congratulate my good friend "Gabby"?

I took my son Lyle along. Lyle was as excited as I was. We managed to get seats directly over the Cardinals' bench. When "Gabby" Street walked out of the Phillies' old Clubhouse in center field, and crossed the diamond carrying the usual big manager's grip, the crowd gave him a big hand. But, if they had known the story "Gabby" told me in secret after the game, every living soul in those stands would have stood up and cheered him like a great hero.

As he approached the Cardinals' bench, I stood up and yelled, "Gabby!"

He looked up, smiled, and shook my hand as I reached down over the railing. I said, "Gabby, I'm Frank Bettger. Remember me from Chattanooga?" With that, this once forgotten man who had suddenly become famous, gave my hand a terrific squeeze. "Frank! How are you doing?" he asked.

"Fine," I assured him. "My son Lyle, here, wants to shake your hand." "Gabby" grabbed Lyle's hand and gave him a grand smile.

I said, "Gabby, I know you must have a wonderful story. Could I see you for a few minutes after the game?"

"Come down to the clubhouse afterward and I'll tell you all about it," he promised.

Two hours later, Lyle and I were sitting with "Gabby" Street in a small, private dressing room. Here is the inspiring story he told us:

"As you know, Frank, I got to drinking. Chattanooga let me go. I began drifting around in small leagues, hittin' the bottle worse all the time. I was going downhill fast. Then one day in a little town in North Carolina, I happened to meet Branch Rickey. He was then general manager of the Cardinals. Branch says: 'Gabby, if you can get hold of yourself and let liquor alone for one year, I've got a job in St. Louis I want you to do for me.'

"One year later I phoned Branch long distance: 'Branch,' I says, 'I haven't touched a drop for one year. Is that job in St. Louis still open for me?'

" 'How soon can you get here?' says Branch.

"Next morning, I'm in Branch's office.

" 'Gabby,' he says, 'I've got an idea.'

"I looks at him a minute, then says, 'Shoot!'

" 'I want you to help me do something that's never been done before. I want you to help me start a baseball farm. Are you interested?'

"Two hours later, Frank, I'm in a Pullman on my way to my first assignment, a small town in a Class D league. It's a good town, but their team is in last place in the league and the fans stopped comin' out. I hang around a couple of days watchin' games, then I go to the owners. They recognize me, wanta know what I'm doin' now. I tell 'em I'm all washed up as a player but would like to buy a club in a small league like this, and manage it.

"These owners were just small merchants in town, sick of putting up more money every two weeks to meet the payroll

for a losin' team. So, I buy the franchise at a low price. They
are tickled pink to unload.

"Next day, I'm back in St. Louis assigning the franchise over
to the Cardinals. Branch ships me a few good young ball players and we start to win. The fans wake up, start comin' out to
see their 'new' ball club and we're soon makin' money.

"Well, Frank, that was the beginning of the 'farm system'
in baseball. After I got a team runnin' good, Branch would
send me on a new assignment. We soon had established a farm
system all around the country."

"How did you happen to become manager of the Cardinals?"
I asked.

"Frank, early this season, I'm back home in Joplin, Missouri,
restin' up between jobs. I'm sittin' in the kitchen with the
Missus—in my stockin' feet, readin' the newspaper. Mom is
cookin' dinner. The phone rings and Mom answers. 'It's a call
from St. Louis for you,' she says, passin' the phone to me. I'm
tilted back on the hind legs of a little wooden chair. 'Yes,' I
says, 'this is Gabby ... what's that? NO! yer kiddin'—yuh
couldn't be serious! ... Sure! I'll be there first thing tomorrow
mornin'!'

"I hang up, lose my balance, pitch backwards over that chair,
phone and all, sprawlin' flat on my face across the kitchen floor.
Mom thinks I dropped dead, starts screamin' and drops a plat-
ter full of fried chicken all over the floor. She leans over me
screamin', 'Gabby! GABBY!'

"I peep up at her out of one eye. She yells: 'What in the
world happened to you?'

" 'I'M MANAGER OF THE ST. LOUIS CARDINALS!' "

Lyle and I laughed and laughed. "Gabby" watched us and

saw tears running down my cheeks. Then he choked up and couldn't go on for a few moments.

"Frank," he continued, looking amazed, as though he was hearing the story himself for the first time, "I was appointed only temporarily as a *fill in*, until they had a chance to pick out the 'right man.' But somehow, from the day I took over, we began to win. At first, everybody thought it was an accident and we'd soon fold up. But we didn't. Now here we are—we've won the pennant! I'm still afraid it's all a dream and I'll wake up and find myself back somewhere in the bush leagues—a down and out drunken hasbeen."

Well, he was too modest to say it, but when "Gabby" Street was Walter Johnson's battery mate in Washington—and the only man who ever caught a ball dropped off the top of Washington Monument!—he was one of the peppiest, most energetic ballplayers in the big leagues. When he took over St. Louis, he began to pump tremendous life and enthusiasm into those potentially great players like Frankie Frisch, "Pepper" Martin, "Chick" Hafey, Jim Bottomley. "Gabby" set them on fire. Nothing could stop them. They went on to win the National League pennant again the following year—then entered the World Series against one of Connie Mack's greatest teams, with Lefty Grove, Mickey Cochrane, Jimmy Foxx, Al Simmons. The betting odds were three to one on the Philadelphia Athletics. But the "A's" were no match for that momentum built up by the "Gashouse Gang." Those Cards overwhelmed the American League Champions, winning four out of six games—and became the *World Champions!* . . .

There was another question I wanted to ask "Gabby." I hesitated, but "Gabby" said, "Go ahead. Anything you wanna ask me."

I said, "Gabby, how were you able to give up liquor after it got such a hold on you?"

"Frank, I just realized there was only *one* solution. *Stop!* Stop right then. I knew there was no other way. That's one fight you don't win in ten or fifteen rounds. *You either win or lose in the first round.* If you can't get by that first drink, you lose ... you're gonna be K.O.'d."

"If you win that first fight," I asked, "is that all? Is that the end of it?"

"Oh, no," grinned Gabby. "The old devil don't give up that easy. He'll be back. With a better approach. And there you are. The gong rings. The fight is on again! What do you do? There's only one way: *lick him in the first round!*"

I wish poor Denny Wolf could have heard that talk. I wish my own father could have heard it. I wish every young man and woman could have heard what "Gabby" Street said that day—and the way he said it!

This is one of the profoundest truths I have ever learned in life: the easiest time to say no, is the *first* time. "Gabby" Street said it much better than I ever could—

"LICK HIM IN THE FIRST ROUND!"

Resolve to perform what you ought; perform without fail what you resolve. RESOLUTION, once become habitual, will keep me firm in my endeavors to obtain all the subsequent virtues.   *Franklin*

In this world, we either discipline ourselves, or we are disciplined by the world. I prefer to discipline myself. Franklin said: "Disobedience is slavery; obedience is *liberty.*"

"Gabby" Street said: "Lick him in the first round!"

The Scriptures say: *He that conquers himself is greater than he that taketh the city.*

Chapter 23

"PAY YOURSELF FIRST"

IT WAS CLAYT HUNSICKER's sixtieth birthday. We had just finished having lunch together. Clayt lit a big birthday cigar, and then made an astounding statement to me. I had never seen him outwardly show any emotion before, but suddenly, his voice seemed to catch in his throat as he said: "I've got a blind bank balance of ten thousand dollars!"

"What is a blind bank balance?" I asked.

"My check book only shows a balance of $2,200, but my actual balance is $12,200. Ten thousand never appears in my checkbook."

I was astonished! For thirty years, Hunsicker had been one of the ten leading salesmen of our company, and recognized nationally; yet, he was known to be perpetually broke. Money flowed through his fingers like sand in an hour glass.

You could see that today was probably the happiest birthday in his life. And I believe I felt almost as thrilled as he was, because Clayt had become like a father to me. I grabbed his hand and shook it heartily as I said, "Congratulations! That's *wonderful!* . . . What are you going to do with that ten thousand dollars?"

"Leave it right where it is!" declared Clayt. "I never want my checking account to get below ten thousand dollars again."

"But, why keep it in a checking account? Why lose the interest on ten thousand dollars?"

"I don't want any interest on it," was his surprising answer.

"Why not?"

"Listen," said Clayt, suddenly on fire, "a man can't have too much confidence in himself. With the kind of confidence that blind balance has given me, I can earn many times the interest I could get on it."

"Wouldn't it give you just as much confidence to take that ten thousand and reduce the mortgage on your home?" I asked.

"I have paid off the entire mortgage on my home. I've paid off everything . . . I don't owe a dollar in the world! *Not a dollar.*"

His voice choked with emotion.

This was astonishing news. I knew his sales had gone way ahead of anything he had ever produced before. But, after all, for thirty years he had broken every resolution he ever made to stop spending faster than he earned.

"Many times," Clayt confessed that day at lunch, "I went home on Friday night without enough money to buy groceries to last us over the weekend. Then, one day about four years ago, something happened to me. I'd been keeping about two jumps ahead of the sheriff; I knew I couldn't keep dodging him much longer; I was fifty-six and my life was more than two-thirds gone.

"All my life I had been paying *everybody* but myself. 'From this day on,' I said to myself, 'I'll *pay myself first*! One third of every dollar I earn, will go into a special account. Whatever is left must see us through!'

"At first, it looked impossible. I owed the bank. I owed the grocer. I owed money everywhere..."

Well! Here was a *new* Clayt Hunsicker I was looking at. By seeing this idea through, he had paid off every dollar he owed in the world. Self-confidence? Enthusiasm? He became *unbeatable*. As one of his clients, a large manufacturer, told me later: "There's no use trying to resist that man. He is the most remarkable salesman I have ever known!"

It seems incredible, but after passing sixty years of age, Hunsicker became a well-to-do man; a leader in his church; a prominent leader in civic activities; and one of the best loved men in his community.

Now I wouldn't want anyone to confuse "Pay Yourself First" with the other priceless lesson Mr. Hunsicker taught me: "Always put your customer *first*; your company *second*; and yourself *last*." ... "Pay Yourself First" refers here to frugality only—a sensible budgeting of our own personal income and expenses. Poor Richard put it this way: "A man may, if he knows not how to save as he gets, keep his nose all his life to the grindstone, and die not worth a groat at last..."

I, myself, had been on a joy ride of spending—creating new obligations so fast that my earnings were always mortgaged ahead. Like Hunsicker, the more I made, the less I had left over for myself.

"Pay Yourself First!" became my *motto*. Not thinking only of myself, but, using this phrase, and telling the Hunsicker story became one of my most motivating closes in selling. That story not only inspired me. I found it inspired others!

Chapter 24

A SHORT CUT TO THE NUTHOUSE

I RECEIVED A SHOCKING LETTER one day from my son Lyle. Lyle was now a Hollywood actor. He wrote the letter "on location," from Sarasota, Florida, where the late Cecil B. DeMille was starting to produce "The Greatest Show on Earth." DeMille had chosen Lyle to play the villain in the picture.

Dear Dad:

The other night, a shabbily dressed man sat at the table next to mine in a small cafeteria. He needed a shave badly, and showed all the earmarks of becoming a bum. He began to talk to me, and I hardly answered more than "yes" or "no." Finally, he said he was from Philadelphia, and wanted to know if I had ever been there. I said "yes," and he asked, "Do you know the such-and-such' building, and the so-and-so' building?" and mentioned several other large mid-city office buildings. I said "yes." He said, "I built them!" I said, "Is that so?" He went on a bit, then asked if I was married and had any children. I said, "Yes." He said, "Let me give you a tip, son. Years ago, an insurance friend of mine sold me $170,000 of life

insurance. I began to drink and gamble in the stockmarket, and, against this insurance man's advice, I gradually cashed in all my policies. My business went to hell,
and I lost everything. You can see what I am now. Get
yourself some life insurance and protect your wife and
kids. Don't ever let it go! Some day, you may wake up
and find it's all for yourself. You know—independence
in your old age."

When I got up to go, he asked my name. I said
"Bettger." He looked positively startled. "Are you related
to Frank Bettger, the fellow who wrote that book, 'From
Failure to Success?' " I said, "Yes, he's my Dad." He ex-
ploded: *"That's the insurance man I was just telling you
about!"* I asked him his name. He said, "Taylor—Bob
Taylor." I asked, "Would you have been the partner of
Harris & Taylor, architects and engineers?" He said,
"That's who I am!"

I guess you realized, Dad, who it was that I was talking
with, long before the end of this story, but I never was
more stunned. He just gets enough work to keep alive
doing odd jobs.

Except for changing the names, everything in this story is
absolutely true. I was shocked to learn of my old friend's plight.
He had been worth almost a million dollars at one time. Yet, I
could understand how he could have got so low. I'll tell you
why:

One brisk September day, as I was leaving the office of a top
executive of a large public utility company, he walked to the
door with me. I knew this man had made a lot of money in
the stockmarket. He put his hand on my shoulder and said,
"Frank, you're a smart fellow. Why don't you make some
money for yourself in the market?"

Was I flattered! It had never occurred to me that *I* was

smart. I thought to myself as I walked down the street, "How could I have been so stupid—if I'm so smart like he says?"

I went to bed that night a poor man. I hadn't lost anything, but I was poor because I was discontented . . . discontented because I knew other people who were making big money so quick and easy.

First thing the next morning, I went to see a friend of mine, a stockbroker. When I told him about my "blind bank balance plan," he laughed at me. He showed me how to multiply my money quickly in companies I had never even heard of before— companies making "phenomenal strides."

He pointed out one company's stock, selling on the market for $11.00 a share. "When the news gets out on what they are doing," he declared, "that stock will go to a hundred by Christmas!"

That night I went to bed a rich man! I had bought four hundred shares of stock in *"big business!"*

Right at that time, I was considering buying an expensive new home in the suburbs, but I was afraid the cost was way over my head. Now, I saw it differently . . . "If I am going to be *rich*, why shouldn't I be *living* among the rich?"

The next morning I phoned the real estate man and made an offer. Within twenty minutes he was in my office with an agreement. I bought that house. The mortgage? It was double anything I anticipated, but I said to myself: "I'll make that up *fast* and pay it all off."

Now, I began getting frequent telephone calls from my stockbroker "friend." He told me about exciting things soon to happen in United Ashcans and Consolidated Gaspipe. I said, "Joe, I just bought a big home on the Main Line. I have no more money to invest."

He said, "You don't need any more money, Frank. You've got plenty of collateral right here!"—So, Joe, let me in on Ashcans and Gaspipe.

The following Monday morning, I was the speaker at our Agency meeting. I was on an emotional jag and tried to impress the men with how *big* I was getting. After the meeting, I was handed an urgent message that my broker friend had been trying to reach me. When I phoned, he said, "Frank, there has been quite a break in the market. Could you get in here before noon with a check?"

I went upstairs to our treasurer's office, and asked him for a pretty stiff advance. He looked surprised. He had just heard my speech. Just then his phone rang. I heard him answer, "Yes, Mr. Bettger is here." He passed the phone to me. It was my broker friend again, and was he excited! "Frank, the market has taken a bad nose-dive since I talked with you. You'd better double that check!"

Well—the panic of 1929 was on. Remember that stock I bought which was going to a hundred by Christmas? It was selling for seventy-five cents by Christmas!

By February, a strong recovery set in. That was my opportunity to get out. Instead, I began feeling *real smart* again. But, within a couple of months, along came the sinking spell. That lasted nearly ten years!

I thought I had an inexhaustible supply of money. I soon found that no sum was inexhaustible. It was like quicksand sucking me down. "Pay *Yourself* First" had been reversed to "Pay Your *Broker* First."

Fear of losing everything made a coward of me. If it hadn't been for my life insurance, I might have gone all to pieces like Bob Taylor, and many others I knew. That boundless enthusiasm for my business lost its bound. I became so ashamed of

my sales production, I didn't want to know the facts, so I
stopped keeping records. That was the *worst* thing I could
have done!

Nobody could get much lower in spirit and more disheart-
ened than I was. I couldn't face my friends, my business asso-
ciates, even my own family. One day, I got to figuring how
much *more* I was worth, dead than alive. My thoughts went
back to the time I stood on the bridge at Chattanooga. I
thought of my little mongrel friend.

I walked out to Fairmount Park, where life for me had its
beginning. I journeyed down Ridge Avenue, past McDaniel's
and Donahue's saloons, and on down to Nassau Street, to the
house where I was born—a four-room, brick, row-house. My
thoughts went back to the early days of my childhood when we
were so poor, we were desperate for just enough food to live
. . . three cents worth of skim milk . . . stale bread . . . corn-meal
mush. I could hear my Mother's voice, teaching us that "to be
wasteful was a *sin*." It seemed more than I could bear, to realize that this same Frank Bettger would gamble and throw his
money away. I had committed a *great sin!* Why? For *what?*
. . . to make money . . . *big money* . . . quick and easy.

Only a stable stood there now. I began to pray. There on
Nassau Street where I was born, *I prayed* . . .

Then I turned the corner and left the rest in God's Hands.
It was now up to Him.

Chapter 25

A STRANGE THING HAPPENS TO ME

I TORE A LEAF OUT OF MY DIARY some time later, and I think I've read it at least once every year since. I probably will continue to read it at least once every year until I go to my grave. Here's what it says:

> BIG EVENT IN MY LIFE!—Received cancelled notes from two banks, stamped *PAID IN FULL!*

Do you know what a pig of lead is? How do you carry a pig of lead? You *don't!* You only lift it onto a truck. If you attempt to carry it, it quickly becomes a dead weight and could almost kill you! I know. I was stupid enough to try it one time when I was a plumber's helper. The boss plumber sent me back to the shop for some tools. I was only a green kid of sixteen at the time; and there was a "smart" clerk in the office, who thought it would be a funny joke to see me try to carry a pig of lead. He said, "Frank, the plumber just phoned and asked me to have you bring him that pig of lead—" (pointing to it over in one corner of the room). It was only about the size of two shoe boxes, end to end. But when I tried to pick it up,

I thought it was nailed to the floor. Somehow, I managed to get that thing up on my shoulder and carry it several city blocks. I've always believed that may have had something to do with my arm going bad in baseball.

Well, my stockmarket experience was like trying to carry a pig of lead. It nearly killed me. When that big executive said to me, "Frank, you're a smart fellow ..." it cost me almost all the money I had saved—all because I was stupid enough to be vulnerable to flattery.

When it came to investing money, Mark Twain, the great American humorist, didn't have any more sense than I had. He was a sucker for all sorts of inventions and lost everything but the kitchen stove. Afterward he wrote: "There are two times a man should not gamble: when he can't afford to gamble; and when he can."

Joe Louis, ex-heavyweight champion of the world, and one of the greatest, put it very well. He said: "... you can't get out, because the more you make, the higher rate is taken out in taxes. It's like doing road work on a treadmill. The faster you run, the faster they move that treadmill against you. No matter how fast you think you're going, you're really not going anywhere at all."

I was on that treadmill for eleven years! This has been a short-cut to the nuthouse for many.

One day, when I was trying to sell a friend of mine more life insurance, he said: "What's the matter with you, Frank? What's happened to you?" I asked him what he meant. He said, "Why, you're beginning to look like so many of the salesmen who come in here. Nine out of ten salesmen who come into my office have a big dollar mark right in the middle of their forehead. I can spot it the minute they walk through that door!"

I was shocked! For I thought I had been keeping my financial situation a dark, deep secret, and didn't know it was showing on me. Yet I had to respect this man, because he was a top sales executive. And he was right! Gambling in the market, I had created so many obligations so fast, that—unknowingly— I was violating the most important principle of all; and selling for my *own* needs, instead of my customers'!

After paying the banks off, I finally worked my way out of debt, and began to make more money than I had ever made before. Then *a strange thing happened* that shaped and determined a new and exciting life for me. It all seemed quite by accident.

By some strange coincidence, I got aboard the same train in New York City that Dale Carnegie was on. Dale was bound for Memphis, Tennessee. I was on my way home to Philadelphia, after a busy day in New York. As the result of our talk on the train that night, Dale and I were soon travelling all over the country together, giving one-week schools in selling and human relations.

At first, I was making talks, as Percy H. Whiting, Dean of the Dale Carnegie Institute, jokingly put it: "on subjects I'd never even heard of before!" But, in a short time, the work became the most exciting adventure of my whole life ... even more exciting than my baseball days! I was elated at the response and enthusiasm shown in these meetings.

One day in Tulsa, Oklahoma, two prominent insurance men invited me to the Tulsa Athletic Club to have lunch with them. They said they were familiar with my record as an insurance man and acted as if they felt sorry for me.

"Frank," said one of the men, "have you gone crazy? Why don't you return to Philadelphia and get back into the life insurance business? You can make more money in one month than you can in this work in a year!"

"Fellows," I answered, "I know this sounds crazy, but a strange thing has happened to me. *I'm not interested any more in making money.*"

For a few moments they just stared blankly at me, then one of them asked: "What *are* you interested in?"

"I'm interested in how I can do the greatest amount of good for the greatest number of people. In this work that I'm doing now, I can reach hundreds of people every night. *Money* never did for me what this work is doing!"

Later in the day, I told Dale about what I said to these men. Dale smiled. "I *knew* you would love this work, Frank. You were made for it. Why don't you start writing a book? You'll write a new kind of book, a book that will be helping and inspiring discouraged young men and women long after you are playing third base in Paradise!"

At first, this sounded fantastic! But in a short time, I *was* writing a book! There is hardly a day that I don't recall Dale's final words to me the last time I saw him on earth:

"... You are on the right track now, Frank. You are *not* preaching. You are telling the story of your life. *Not* just the typical American success story, but the unusual story of the successful idea and methods you developed in your life—which made your story possible. ..."

The day I received word over the telephone that he had died after a lingering illness, I sat down and cried. ...

"If you would be *free*, think of *saving* as well as *getting*; away then with your expensive follies, and you will not then have much cause to complain of hard times and heavy taxes. As Poor Richard says, 'The second Vice is lying, the first is running into debt. And lying rides upon debt's back.' Preserve your freedom; maintain your independence; be frugal and free . . . this doctrine, my friends, is reason and wisdom. Profit by this wisdom."

Pay yourself first.

Chapter 26

THE LIE DETECTOR TEST

ONE YEAR WHEN I WAS PRESIDENT of the Ben Franklin Club in Philadelphia, we had Professor A. K. Van Tine of the Drexel Institute of Technology, a Lie-Detector expert, speak at one of our annual Ladies' Night dinners, and demonstrate the machine. He was highly entertaining and as clever with his questions and cross-examinations as any trial lawyer I have ever heard.

He gave several demonstrations of how he could determine whether our answers were true or false. If I hadn't taken part in one of them myself, I doubt whether I could have believed it wasn't "rigged."

Two ladies and two men, selected at random, left the dining room and sauntered out into the lobby. I was one of the two men. The other man made an out-of-town, person-to-person phone call from one of the pay station phone booths. The operator reported that the party he called was not at home. We knew this in advance, because that party was attending our meeting!

The operator returned the quarter, but the man doing the phoning intentionally left the money in the coin box. Then both ladies, one at a time, entered the booth and pretended to take the money. I did the same thing. One of us *did* take the coin.

When all four of us returned to the banquet room, no one knew who had the quarter—except the one who really took it.

Well, it proved to be a lot of fun—positively exciting—how cleverly Professor Van Tine questioned each of us separately. All four of us firmly denied removing the quarter from the coin box, or had any idea who was the guilty party. With a strong light directed on the machine, everyone in the crowd could plainly see two pens fluctuating, as the "suspect's" blood pressure and respiration changed in response to the questions and cross-examination.

The irregular movements up and down were being recorded on graph paper moving slowly around a drum. The expert was keeping a "blow by blow" score. By the rapt attention of our gathering, one might have thought he was trying to find a murderer!

Finally, the score added up to one *unmistakable* conclusion: Prof. Van Tine pointed to *me* and said: "*There* is the guilty party!" ... and to the utter amazement of everybody, he was *right!*

The demonstration was followed by a highly interesting open question-and-answer period. This expert said, "To operate the Lie Detector successfully, requires considerable skill, which comes only with long practice and experience. Yet, nearly everybody," he declared, "possesses some degree of 'lie-detector' instinct."

I knew what he meant. In my early days of selling, I worked a couple of days a week as "bird dog" for Clayt Hunsicker. I wanted to see him *perform!* I wanted to hear exactly what he said to people, and what he did, that made him one of the most successful salesmen in the country. I soon found out one of the

most important reasons . . . When Mr. Hunsicker walked into
a man's office, I was conscious of some kind of hidden power
he possessed. The man we went to see seemed instantly prepared to accept whatever Hunsicker might say to him—before
Clayt spoke a word! It was his character and personality that
created the favorable atmosphere. He had that strength of
character to be true, when no one else would know the difference!

. . . Believing in this philosophy cost me a big job one time.
It happened only a few days after the Ben Franklin Club
Ladies' Night dinner I told about. A prosperous building
contractor, who had become a large client of mine, took me
over to City Hall by definite appointment to see a man he said
was " 'Boss' of the City."

Imagine my surprise when the 'boss' was not the Mayor, but
the real power behind a political machine!

But can you imagine my astonishment when these men said
they were going to make ME Mayor of Philadelphia!

Me! a "sixth grader," with no political experience, no executive training whatever, Mayor of the third largest city in the
United States!

"Why do you want to make *me* Mayor?" I asked them.

"Because we can elect you," the Big Boss answered quietly
and deliberately. "You were a poor boy, came from a poor
family, and you've come up the hard way . . . first a failure in
business . . . now an outstanding success! Yes sir, you've got
the perfect success story. We can elect you by a large majority!"

I said, "You've picked the wrong man."

"What do you mean?" asked the Big Boss, surprised.

"If I should be elected Mayor of Philadelphia, I would have
to represent the people! I wouldn't permit any political machine to tell me what to do!"

I knew by the way both men looked and acted, they *believed* I was *sincere*! They didn't need a lie detector to know whether I was telling the truth.

... That was the *first* time they approached me. And that was the *last*!"

In 1920, the famous Federal Judge, Kenesaw Mountain Landis, was induced to retire from the bench and become high commissioner of professional baseball. His salary was set at $40,000 a year as "Czar" of American Baseball. If they had paid Judge Landis a million dollars, it would have been a good investment.

He was an absolutely fearless man, with the reputation of complete fairness. Judge Landis first attracted nation-wide attention as Federal Judge by fining one of the most powerful oil companies in America $29,240,000 for accepting freight rebates.

Shortly after being appointed "Czar" he became faced with baseball's worst scandal! Truth began to leak out about the 1919 World Series between the Chicago White Sox and the Cincinnati Red Legs being "fixed." It was discovered that a big gambling syndicate had bribed enough star White Sox players to "throw" the series!

When the series opened the betting odds rated Chicago 10 to 1 to beat the comparatively weak Cincinnati Red Legs, the White Sox, that year, being classed as one of the greatest teams ever put together.

But, to the astonishment of millions of baseball fans, the Red Legs overwhelmed the White Sox, beating them five out of eight games!

Now came the famous Chicago trial, so masterfully conducted by Judge Landis. Eight great White Sox stars were convicted and became known as the "Black Sox." They were banished from organized baseball for life!

This sensational event put professional baseball on trial, threatening the major leagues with disgrace and possible decline. But that trial turned out to be a blessing in disguise! Judge Landis proved that the great national game was one business the racketeers could not touch! And it established baseball as an example of the *highest* principles of our American way of life.

SUMMED UP

Use no hurtful deceit; think innocently and justly, and, if you speak, speak accordingly.

—Franklin

Have the strength of character to be true when no one else will know the difference.

Chapter 27

HOW TO DESTROY AN ENEMY

AFTER A FEW MINUTES' pleasant conversation, a friend I happened to meet on the street one morning, lowered his voice and asked: "Frank, what kind of fellow is this Joe Doakes? He's connected with your company, isn't he?"

"Yes, he is," I answered.

"I never liked that guy," he confided. "Is he the big shot he tries so hard to make everybody think he is?"

Now there *was* a time when I would have welcomed an opportunity to tell some of the unfavorable things I heard about this fellow Joe Doakes—and felt justified in doing it. I never had been able to make friends with him. More than once, people told me he had made uncomplimentary remarks about me. We were always polite to each other, but there was something about me he didn't like. I don't know what it was, but I always felt as though we were uncomfortable in each other's presence.

Well—instead of saying anything unfavorable, I told my friend all the *good* things I *knew* about Joe ... that he was a wonderful family man; a tremendous worker; a great scholar of his business; and one of the most able salesmen in our organization.

My friend seemed quite surprised, but acted as though he was glad to change his opinion of Joe.

I never did hear what happened, but there could be no doubt about it, what I said got back to Joe. Within a few days, he walked into my office. I invited him to sit down, but he said he couldn't, he had an appointment. It just seemed that he wanted to have a friendly little chat. That strained tension between us was *definitely* gone!

After he left, I thought, "Now that's a strange thing. It's been years since he has been in my office."

Shortly afterward, he brought his wife in late one afternoon. "This is Mom's night off," he said, laughing, "so I'm taking her to dinner and the movies." His wife had never been in my office before, but we had a delightful conversation. From that day on, Joe and I gradually became warm friends.

I shudder, and am ashamed to think how at one time I allowed myself to become infected with that vile, cancerous disease . . . *criticizing others.* Even carrying unfavorable news about people! I don't know how I could have been so stupid and blind to the consequences of "T.M.T."–too much talk! The vicious result, I found, was that it was almost certain to get back to the other person–and never just the way it was said!

The truth of this was never brought to light more convincingly than it was one night when I was taking the public speaking course. Dale Carnegie took one of the students out into the hallway and told him a short human interest story. That student in turn called another one out, and repeated the story to him. In this way, it was relayed to each one present–about thirty-five of us. In the meantime, class was going on as usual.

Then—while the last man was out of the room having the story told to him—Mr. Carnegie repeated the story to the rest of the class as he had *originally* told it to the first student.

Now came the fun!

Those last two men were called back into the room, and the final man to hear the story repeated it to the entire group. What he told was so *completely* different from the original version, it threw the whole class into uproarious laughter. The only *true* thing left in the story—was a horse!

What struck all of us so funny, was the surprised expression on this man's face. He violently protested that he repeated the story *precisely* the way it was told to him! And there is no question but what he thought he did. But everybody else declared likewise! It was impossible to fix the blame on anyone . . .

A prominent Catholic priest recently said: "I have heard people confess to breaking every one of the Ten Commandments—except 'Thou shalt not bear false witness against thy neighbor'—yet, this is the one we all break most often."

Benjamin Franklin discovered the best way to destroy an enemy: *"I will speak ill of no man . . . and speak all the good I know of everybody."*

I tried this principle in business and found one of the quickest ways to win and hold the confidence of others is to:

PRAISE YOUR COMPETITORS!

I have been in Kansas City, Missouri, many times over the years, but never got to know that great city's remarkable mayor, H. Roe Bartle, on his own home grounds. I did have the good fortune, however, to meet him in San Juan, Puerto Rico recently, where my wife and I were taking a short vacation.

Once you meet Roe Bartle, you will never forget him! For

one thing, he is one of the biggest men I've ever met—a "full" 290 lbs. . . . over 6 ft. tall . . . and possesses a full-sized heart to match.

We found out *why* the people of Kansas City love and cherish him so much. It might be summed up with a little story he told us while we were sitting together talking and enjoying the magnificent view from the terrace of the lovely Caribe Hilton Hotel, looking out over the blue Caribbean Sea.

Roe said: "I used to keep a 'little black book.' I entered in it the names of every person who ever double-crossed me, or said anything about me I didn't like. I kept this record to make sure I would get *even* with every one of them some day!

"Then, one time I came across these words of the great Will Rogers: 'I never met a man I did not like.' This phrase *haunted* me. I had always considered myself a religious man. But suddenly those words made me realize that my little black book was a *symbol of hate!* That black book had to go! And the hate in *me* had to go with it—before I was to get my life right with God!"

Mayor Bartle said, just this *one idea* he got from Will Rogers opened up a whole new world of *happiness* for him; and won more friends for him in one year than his little black book would have won in a lifetime.

Will Rogers is generally thought of as a humorist, but he was something far greater than that. In his time, he was possibly the most popular man in America. What made him so popular was not so much his ability to tell a good story, or to skip a rope . . . It was his great talent for making people *happy!*

Will was proud of his Cherokee Indian ancestry. He once said: "My folks didn't come over on the Mayflower, but when the Mayflower landed, we were there to meet them!" . . .

Shortly after we met Roe Bartle in San Juan, my wife and I

made a trip to Tulsa, Oklahoma. We took a run over to Clare-
more, Will Rogers' old stamping grounds, afterward, stopping
at the Will Rogers Hotel. The next morning, we spent a couple
of inspiring hours out at the Will Rogers Memorial. We must
have stood a full five minutes in complete silence before that
great bronze statue by Jo Davidson of the man with the wonderful, warm-hearted smile! We never really understood the
meaning of that smile, until we read and reread the inscription
at its base:

"I NEVER MET A MAN I DIDN'T LIKE."

Chapter 28

"YER YELLOW!"

Back in the days shortly after I joined the St. Louis Cardinals, we appeared in Boston, Massachusetts, to play the Braves. I was particularly excited about playing there and could hardly wait until I got out on the field. *There was a reason.*

I had never been in Boston before, but I *had* been in Haverhill—some thirty miles away, and had played on the Haverhill team, in the New England League. The manager, Billy Hamilton, was a former big-leaguer and one of the really great players. But, as a manager, Billy was a hot-headed Irishman who drove his players with criticism and fear. From the first day I joined them, he found fault with everything I did. The third day, a big, handsome pitcher from Mobile, Alabama, joined us. Although he had been travelling on trains for twenty-four hours, the manager put him in to pitch immediately after his arrival.

Well, it seemed like every other ball this fellow pitched was hit down to short-stop. And you guessed it—I was playing short-stop! The ground was pretty rough and balls bounced off my shins and chest, and head. I was only charged with four errors, but I must have had eight!

152

I never heard such violent language as that manager handed out to me and the new pitcher. I got so confused, I couldn't do anything right, and the pitcher was almost as bad. We lost the game 14 to 3.

That night I couldn't eat. While the players were having dinner, I stood out in front of the hotel trying to think what I should do. Soon, out came the manager. He didn't see me. He walked over to the curb and leaned against an awning pole. He didn't look as though he had eaten either.

Gradually, the other players came out—but steered clear of the manager. Finally, out walked the big, handsome, southerner who pitched that day. But he wasn't the worrying kind. He had put away a tremendous meal and was feeling very well satisfied, picking the remains of a turkey dinner from his teeth.

Strolling over to the manager he said with a broad smile: "Well, Billy, I was a *way off* today, wasn't I?" "Yes, and you'll be a damned sight further off tomorrow!" snapped Billy.

And he was!

That night, I went to Billy Hamilton and handed him my uniform. "What's this?" he asked. "I'm through," I replied, almost in a whisper.

"Forget it!" said he. "Get out there tomorrow and show 'em whatcha kin do."

"I couldn't," I told him. "If I went out there tomorrow, I wouldn't be able to catch a ball."

"*Yer yellow!*" snarled Billy . . .

I took the first train out of Haverhill the next morning. The president of the club had given me my unconditional release.

. . . So, Billy Hamilton must have been one of the most surprised men in baseball when he saw my name not so long afterward, appearing in the line-up, playing with the St. Louis

Cardinals! That first time we played in Boston, I just *know* Billy took the thirty-three mile trip down from Haverhill, to see with his own eyes if I were the same "busher" he tied a can to for being "*Yellow!*" I didn't actually see him, I was afraid to look up into the stands because I knew it would upset me. But I definitely could *feel* he was there, somewhere in the crowd.

I intended to skip this bitter experience with Billy Hamilton. In fact, I always wanted to forget it, and have never mentioned it to anyone until now. But it did have an important bearing on my life.

Disheartening as those three days in Haverhill were to me, my first three days with the Cardinals *could* have been worse! The first day, I struck out on *one pitched ball!* . . . Two days later, we arrived in Pittsburgh. They had just completed building Forbes Field, the first all steel and concrete stadium in the big leagues. The players told me, "We're not gonna play Pittsburgh . . . we're gonna play *Hans Wagner!*" And they were not exaggerating. That's the way they all felt about this great player!

Bresnahan put me in to play short-stop. This was my first *full* game with St. Louis. In the seventh inning, the score stood 3 to 2, in our favor. Wagner was on first base, and Tommy Leach, another great baserunner, was on third. On the first pitched ball, Wagner decided to steal second. Phelps, catching for us that day, made a perfect throw. I caught the ball at second base and almost laughed at how easy Wagner was making it for me . . . he *stopped!* I looked at him a moment . . . reached out to touch him . . . but he backed away . . . *then*, to my bewilderment, began trotting slowly *back to first base!* This didn't make sense to me. I glanced at Leach over on third base. He was standing relaxed, with both feet on top of the bag,

arms folded. So I made a *sudden dash* at Wagner, reaching out
to tag him! . . . Then I discovered why they called him the
"Flying Dutchman!" As soon as we got going full speed, Leach
dashed like crazy *for home!* Without even slowing down, I
heaved the ball to cut Leach off at the home plate. That ball
didn't come within twenty feet of the catcher. It shot like a
bullet straight into the concrete players' bench where about
ten extra Cardinal players were leisurely stretched out watching the game. Before they could scramble out to safety, the
ball bounded back and forth from every angle, barely missing
their heads, but finally landing *flush on Bresnahan's jaw!*

My throw cleared the bases and settled that game. And I
thought it settled *me* too!

After the inning finally ended, Bresnahan nodded for me to
come over to him. He made room on the bench for me to sit
next to him. "Do you know what you did wrong?" he asked
quietly.

"Yes."

"What?" . . . He was watching me closely.

"Running full speed like that, I should have thrown the ball
to Konetchy (our first baseman). Koney could have thrown
Leach out at home easily."

"Right!" grinned Bresnahan, giving me a friendly pat on the
back.

. . . Roger Bresnahan might have ruined me that day for his
team, if he had given me the Billy Hamilton treatment. From
that day on, I would have broken a leg to help win a game
for him!

To believe in a man is the first step toward helping him.

Miller Huggins, captain of the team, had a wonderful formula for boosting the morale of his men. He always had a
vision of each player when he was going at his best. Then,

when the inevitable slump came, instead of criticizing, Huggins recalled the picture of the player when he was at his best—and tried to get that picture over to the man. It worked! I'm sure this formula had something to do with Huggins later being chosen manager of the New York Yankees, and with the great success he had in New York.

During my years in baseball, I never saw criticism do anything but harm to ballplayers. But I did see *praise and encouragement* make stars out of ordinary players. I saw it produce harmony and a fighting spirit on teams of ordinary players that carried them on to win championships!

1. The best way to destroy an enemy:—Apply the Principle of one of the world's greatest diplomats, Benjamin Franklin: *I will speak ill of no man—and speak all the good I know of everybody.*

2. Everybody likes to feel important. People are hungry for praise—*not flattery*—but *honest, sincere* appreciation.

3. During my years in baseball, I never saw criticism do anything but harm to ballplayers. But, I saw honest praise and encouragement make stars out of ordinary players. After retiring from baseball, I saw these principles produce the same results in *business*—and in the *home!*

Chapter 29

THE AMERICAN PEOPLE'S NUMBER ONE
INTEREST

IF YOU WERE ASKED to name what you consider to be the "first essential for successful living," what would be *your* answer? Chicago University wanted to get the American people's answer to this question so they spent two years conducting a nation-wide survey. By an *overwhelming* majority, it showed that the number one interest of adults is *"Health!"*

What *is* the health of American people? *Mortality* statistics say that America is extremely healthy; for example, during recent years the life expectancy has increased twenty years—from age forty-nine to sixty-nine. But, can health be measured by mortality statistics *only?* Our crowded hospitals and sanitariums and nursing homes give us a different answer. Let's look at the facts:

Most of the increase in life expectancy is due to lower death rates in infants and children. The medical profession has achieved phenomenal results in reducing contagious diseases like diphtheria, typhoid, scarlet-fever, smallpox, polio, etc. At the same time, however, degenerative diseases like cancer, heart disease, diabetes, etc., continue to increase at an alarming rate.

Health—for many years—was my number one problem. I was an invalid child from birth, and spent the most part of my first years indoors looking out at the other children at play, and contracted *every* form of children's diseases except smallpox. Neighbors said to my mother, "Mame, you'll never raise that boy. It's killing you taking care of him and doing all this other work too." But Mother always told them: "The doctor says if I can raise Frank to *sixteen* he'll probably live to a pretty good age." Neighbors would say, "Yes, but Mame, *you'll* never make it yourself!" But Mother did make it—'til she was eighty-three. And here I am seventy-two looking forward to the next ten years as the most important years of my life!

When I was twelve, a surprising thing happened to me. The famous Eugene Sandow, world's strongest man, came to Keith's Theatre, Philadelphia. They announced that at special Saturday matinee Sandow would explain how he raised himself from an invalid boy to the world's strongest man!

This I couldn't miss! I sat up in the "peanut gallery." I could hardly wait to see Sandow. "Hats Off!" yelled a big cop in the rear, pounding his club on the floor. Out went the lights! Up went the curtain. . . . And *out walked Sandow!*

He was spectacular in skin tights and had the most perfect physique I have ever seen. I listened with wild excitement as he told how his father had taken him in a wheel chair to a theatre in Berlin to see a "strong man" perform. The man had cured himself from disease by a simple method of progressive exercises. Sandow said he became inspired that night. He demonstrated those exercises, and made a big point of how he kept thinking thoughts of faith and courage during his exercise periods. Sandow looked up to the "peanut" and I thought he looked straight at me as he said, "If I could do it, *you* can do it!" Tears streamed down my cheeks. I went home that night with new hope—a determination to become a healthy man as Sandow did.

Immediately after school each day I went home and followed Sandow's instructions. I continued them religiously for years. I never aspired to become a "strong man." I just wanted to be as strong as the "Swampoodle Gang" who used to beat up all the other kids in the schoolyard.

A year later I was able to take a newspaper route serving papers from five to seven every morning. At eighteen I became a professional ballplayer. In addition to the physical benefits, I've always believed the *self-discipline* of performing those exercises every day had much to do with my persistence to follow through, years later, with Franklin's Thirteen Weeks' Plan.

Although this boyhood experience is intended mainly for the younger generation, the balance of this chapter is intended for *everyone* from eight to eighty.

One day I read in the newspaper about a man in New York named Fletcher who had become famous. This man had suffered with an advanced case of stomach ulcers and couldn't retain the simplest food in his stomach. He actually was starving to death.

But Fletcher cured himself by chewing each mouthful of food until, he said, it looked like milk and actually tasted *sweet*! After reaching *fifty*, Fletcher astounded the medical profession and the sports world by making the *American Olympic Team*! He established records in shot-putting and weight lifting. His rule for a *normal* person was to chew each mouthful thirty-two times. This became widely known as "*Fletcherizing*" your food.

Probably no other boy would have bothered with such a thing except one who was handicapped from birth with health problems. I have been "Fletcherizing" now for nearly sixty years. Nobody could enjoy food more than I do. I eat everything and have never been troubled with indigestion.

After I became a ballplayer I heard much talk about players "Drinking" themselves out of the big leagues. I did see that happen with a few, but for everyone who drank himself out, there were probably ten who *ate* themselves out!

Chewing each mouthful thirty-two times—"Fletcherizing"—simply means using common sense about masticating our food properly. It is almost impossible to *overeat*; it increases the flow of saliva and you are never troubled with indigestion or ulcers. It helps maintain normal weight. I have remained approximately the same weight for fifty years and never diet. Franklin wrote: *"I saw few die from hunger—of eating, a hundred thousand."*

Insurance records prove that overweight from overeating shortens life. The death rate from all causes is 22 per cent higher for people who are 5 to 14 per cent overweight. Among people who are 25 per cent overweight, mortality is *75 per cent higher*!

While serving newspapers one morning, I saw a large picture on the front pages of Bob Fitzsimmons who the night before knocked out Jim Corbett winning the world's heavyweight championship. Corbett weighed 195 pounds and Fitzsimmons only 160. This amazing fighter had now become middleweight, light-heavyweight, and heavyweight champion of the world!

Many experts declared that Fitz was no doubt the most powerful puncher in boxing history. Interviewed after the fight, Fitzsimmons was asked if there was some hidden secret to his terrific power. He had such a surprising answer, it was featured on the front pages: Fitz said, "Yes there is. The power comes from the chief muscle of the body—the *diaphragm*."

"Would you explain *how*?" they all wanted to know.

"*Abdominal* breathing develops that power," declared Fitz. "If you blow your breath into a paper bag, the air goes right to the bottom and expands the bag from the bottom up. Most people are *chest* breathers. They inhale and exhale from the top of the lungs. Oxygen seldom gets down into the lower lung cells. Abdominal breathing forces the diaphragm up and down increasing the supply of oxygen in the blood, at the same time aids the circulation of the blood, somewhat the same principle as the way expanding and contracting of the arteries shares the work of the heart."

From the beginning, when I tried this I could feel a "*lift*" right down to a tingling in my finger tips. Although doctors said I was born with a bad heart, over the years, insurance companies have sold me all the life insurance I could pay for —at *standard* rates.

I'm convinced that abdominal breathing is the correct way to breathe. It's natural. I've noticed animals, even in their sleep, breathe that way.

How important is correct breathing to the heart and circulatory system? Well, I just read in the Journal of the Heart Association of Pennsylvania this astounding fact: "More people have been lost in the United States in one year through heart and circulatory diseases than in all the wars in which this country has been engaged!"

As I've grown older, I find myself taking less formal exercise but doing more and more *stretching*. It is an easy and most enjoyable form of exercise, takes so little time, that it is being practiced by some of the busiest people in America.

I became sold on it when Hugh Fullerton, famous sports-writer went to Chicago years ago to interview Frank Gotch, from Des Moines, Iowa. Frank was preparing to wrestle world's champion Zybysko, "The unbeatable" giant Pole. Fuller-ton went to Gotch's hotel room and found Frank lying in bed in shorts. He, . . . well let's listen to Hugh tell it himself:

"Hello!" greeted Gotch. "Sit down a minute 'til I finish my workout."

All I could see him do was stretch various parts of his body, relax, then stretch again. Suddenly Gotch leaped out of bed, grabbed me—I weighed 165—tossed me into the air, caught me and plumped me down into a chair, laughing!

"What's the idea?" I asked, really frightened.

"My workout!" explained Gotch. "Now all I need is to learn to call that big guy a this—and that—in Polish and I'm in condition!"

"When do you go to the gym, and out on the road to train?"

"I *don't*," replied Gotch. "Let the other fellow wear himself out on the road. I've seen too many good men leave their fight out on the road."

"Quit kidding," I remarked. "How do you keep yourself in such marvelous condition?"

"All I need is *stretching!*"

"Stretching?"

"Yes. Ever watch a dog or a cat get up after a sleep? It stretches every muscle in its body, just as I was doing when you came in. Cats and dogs usually keep in pretty good condition. Right?"

"Two nights later I saw Frank Gotch enter the ring with a panther like step. And, almost without panting, throw the 'un-beatable' giant Pole *twice*, and win the world's wrestling championship!"

Hugh Fullerton's story *convinced* me. I became a confirmed
S T R E T C H E R !

Much of my stretching is done in bed before I get up morn-
ings. Also, at odd moments during the day—only for a couple
of minutes. I love to take a "seventh-inning stretch" like the
crowd does at the ballgame! If I don't have time for a short
nap before dinner, I stretch out on the floor a few minutes,
sort of a "do-it-yourself" spine-straightening osteopathy!

You no doubt are saying to yourself: "This fellow Bettger
made heroes out of men with strong backs and weak minds!"
Well, Ben Franklin had a strong back, but he also had a pretty
wonderful mind. Remember? And Ben wrote a lot about how
to maintain good health. In fact, *four* of his thirteen principles
were largely health measures.

Reader's Digest quoted Dr. Paul Dudley White, noted heart
specialist as saying: "I believe that the physiological effect of
exercise throughout one's life will probably, in time, be proved
one of the best antidotes against the alarming development
of the epidemic of coronary thrombosis and high blood pressure.
Along with exercise, of course, there should be recognition of
the wisdom of preventing overweight, and of avoiding rich
food heavy with animal fat."

. . . How long has health been the *Number One* interest of
people? Well, 1900 years before Jesus ever knew of the Chicago University's survey, He devoted a great portion of His
three years' ministry on earth to healing the sick. Many of the
Old Hebrew Laws and the Ten Commandments, written more
than a thousand years before the time of Christ, are *basically*
health laws.

Food:

Chew each mouthful 32 times. You'll double one of the greatest pleasures in life; you'll be free from indigestion; you will maintain your normal weight and *live longer!*

Exercise:

Try to get some form of exercise daily. But avoid excess or violent activities after forty. One of the most beneficial forms of exercise is a good, luxurious S-T-R-E-T-C-H before getting out of bed in the morning; a "seventh inning" stretch a couple of times each day only takes a few moments. Improves your posture, keeps you *supple* and *fit!*

Rest Frequently:

If possible, take a twenty minute nap before evening dinner or after lunch. Relax often. Loosen collar, shoes and belt when taking a nap or sitting for a long while. Change shoes for slippers when home; many men are now doing this in the office.

Health Examination:

We have compulsory car inspection laws for safety and longer life of the car. Why not apply the same common sense to the *human* machine? Have a complete medical check-up once a year, dentist check-up every six months; likewise eyes tested every couple of years.

Chapter 30

THE SHOT GUN BANQUET

REMEMBER IN THE BEGINNING OF THE BOOK I told about the "most fantastic ballgame ever played anywhere?"

Well, several years later, I was surprised to receive an invitation to attend the annual banquet given by the Delaware County League in Chester. I decided not to attend because I was determined to quit playing ball and devote all my time and energy to my business. I had already resigned as coach at Swarthmore College.

But then my old friend, Vernon Touchstone, phoned and asked me if I was going to the "Shot Gun Banquet." I asked him what he meant? Vernon said, "That guy who broke up our final play-off game at Clifton Heights with the shot gun is gonna be there, and demonstrate how he shot that ball in mid-air. All the other players will be there. There'll be plenty of excitement!"

This I couldn't miss.

Well, the banquet was a sell-out, double the size crowd of any they ever had before. But the shot gun guy never showed up. Instead, we saw a surprise performance that, I'm sure, few of us have ever forgotten.

The principal speakers were John K. Tener, Governor of the State of Pennsylvania, and former president of the National Baseball League, also William I. Schaffer, Chief Justice of the Supreme Court of the State. This really was big league stuff!

However, those speakers were *not* the big surprise. Each manager of the four Delaware County League teams was called on to say just a "few words." But when it came to Bill Miller's turn, manager of Upland, Bill rose and humbly confessed that he couldn't talk before a crowd but his friend, Ben Ludlow, would speak for him. Mr. Ludlow was a young lawyer. Before that night, no one had ever heard of him.

Well, Sir, that young attorney *stole the show!* What the Governor and the Chief Justice said, probably was soon forgotten. Ben Ludlow's talk has lived with me *always*. He spoke only five minutes—he was terrific! The thing that made such a deep and lasting impression on me was his wonderful contagious smile. Ben just radiated happiness, and quickly had everybody else looking and feeling happy. He did something I never saw any speaker do before. He continued that wonderful smile all through his talk.

I was so impressed with the effect he had on that crowd, I determined to emulate Ben Ludlow's smile all the rest of my life, whether I was talking to one person or a thousand. I soon found that I became more welcome everywhere when I did this.

What happened to the young attorney who had such a magical effect on the audience that night—the crowd which went there to see a fight? Benjamin Ludlow rapidly became one of the most successful and widely known lawyers in Pennsylvania, and one of the best loved men in the State.

When the "Four-Minute-Men" organization was formed by the Government during World War One, who do you think

12

was appointed its head in Pennsylvania? Right! That young lawyer with the warmhearted, contagious smile. When Ben Ludlow stood up at our meetings and inspired us to carry the messages of liberty and victory to our people, he set us on fire. One minute he had everybody smiling, the next minute he jerked tears from us; but Ben kept smiling right through the tears in his own eyes.

Now, I don't want to give anyone the impression that I think happiness consists merely of a smile—but I have found this. It is a wonderful *self-starter*! A smile didn't come easy for me at first. After my father died, I saw my wonderful mother working every day from five o'clock in the morning 'til midnight to keep us all together in our little home. During those terrible epidemic years in the "gay nineties," three of my four sisters died. We got so we were *afraid* to smile. We actually came to believe it would bring us bad luck if we acted too happy!

But I learned this: when you are low in spirit, if you *force* yourself to sit up and smile,—just the mere physical action of *acting* happy, will tend to make you happy! This is an idea actually proven through years of experimenting by one of America's most famous psychologists and philosophers, Professor William James of Harvard.

This minute—are you worrying? I know this may sound ridiculous. SMILE! You cannot worry and smile, both at the same time. Try it. It is impossible! You will either stop one or the other.

Will you try it? Try it every day just for this week. Give every living soul you meet the *best* smile you ever smiled in your life—even your own wife and children—and see how much better you *feel* and *look*! It is one of the best ways I know to "stop worrying and start living." See how much more welcome you feel wherever you are, wherever you go.

The Origin of Thanksgiving Day in America

(A Good Message for Families to read aloud together on Thanksgiving Day)

"There is a tradition that, in the planting of New England, the Settlers met with many Difficulties and Hardships as is generally the case when a civilized People attempt establishing themselves in a wilderness Country. Being piously disposed, they sought Relief from Heaven, by laying their Wants and Distresses before the Lord, in frequent set Days of Fasting and Prayer. Constant Meditation and Discourse on these Subjects kept their Minds gloomy and discontented; and, like the Children of Israel, there were many disposed to return to that Egypt, which Persecution had induced them to abandon. At length, when it was proposed in the Assembly to proclaim another Fast, a Farmer of plain Sense arose, and remarked that the *Inconvenience they suffered, and concerning which they had so often wearied Heaven with their complaints, were not so great as they might have expected*, and were *diminishing* every day, as the Colony strengthened; that the Earth began to reward their Labor, and to furnish liberally for their substance; that the Seas and Rivers were full of Fish, the Air sweet, the Climate healthy; and above all, that they were there in the full Enjoyment of Liberty, civil and religious. He therefore thought, that reflecting and conversing on these subjects would be more comfortable, as tending more to make them contented with their situation; and that it would be more becoming the Gratitude they owed to the Divine Being, if, instead of a *Fast*, they should proclaim a *Thanksgiving*. His Advice was taken; and from that day to this they have, in every Year, observed circumstances of public Felicity sufficient to furnish Employment for a Thanksgiving Day; which is therefore constantly ordered and religiously observed."

—B. FRANKLIN

Summed Up

The most common prayer: "Lord, help me"!
The most uncommon prayer: "Thank you, Father."

Be not disturbed at trifles, or accidents common
or unavoidable.
—FRANKLIN

Give every living soul you meet the *best* SMILE you
ever SMILED in your life. It is one of the best
ways to stop worrying, and start living!

Great beauty, great strength, and great riches,
are really and truly of no great use. A right
heart exceeds all.
—FRANKLIN

Chapter 31

A TREMENDOUS THOUGHT

THE UNTIMELY DEATH of Walter LeMar Talbot, president of The Fidelity Mutual Life Insurance Company some years ago was a sad and great loss to the organization. Mr. Talbot was going to be a very difficult man for anyone to follow. The Board of Directors consulted several top officers of other large companies. Three of them said, "E. A. Roberts, vice-president of The Minnesota Mutual Life Insurance Company, is just the man you are looking for."

In a short time, Mr. Roberts was on his way East to become president of the Fidelity.

It didn't take long to discover that one of Mr. Roberts' greatest assets was his complete humility. For instance, during the first few weeks while his family was making the necessary preparations for moving from St. Paul, Minnesota, to Philadelphia, Pennsylvania, the new president made his temporary living quarters at the Barclay Hotel in the center of town. Each morning, instead of taking a taxicab out to the Head Office, located on the Benjamin Franklin Parkway, he rode there in a trolley car, where he was sure to meet many of the company's employees, mostly the clerks. He always sat beside one of them, laughed and talked with everybody around him, just like one of them. When they all got off the trolley car, he walked up the street with them to the entrance facing Fairmount Park. He was a big man, but he ran up the twenty-five steps, opened one of the big doors to the imposing entrance of the building, and *held the door open* until everyone else entered! Now, the employees stepped aside for the president to enter the elevator and ride up alone—the usual custom in those days for presidents of large institutions. . . . Not this new president! "Get in, everybody!" he invited laughingly; then he squeezed in with them.

When the Company held an informal reception for him in their auditorium, they closed down business at 3:30 P.M. I had just returned from an extended tour around the country, and was there for the occasion. Every employee, executive officer, and many salesmen as well, crowded in, anxious to hear E. A. Roberts' speech. That "E" stands for Ellsworth. He was properly introduced, then started his speech like this: "I am 6 feet 2 inches tall, and weigh 220 pounds, and I can lick any man in the room. . . ."

An immediate roar went up from the crowd, drowning out the new president's voice. One employee stood up. He was 6 ft. 7 inches tall! Mr. Roberts raised one hand for attention— "You didn't let me finish," he protested . . . "I can lick any man in this room who calls me Ellsworth! . . . Call me 'Bob.'"

Then "Bob" asked us a question: "How many of you here have ever been in the president's office?"

A great majority failed to raised their hands.

"We'll fix that today," he said. "I'm going back there in a few minutes, and I want every one of you to come in and shake hands with me. And, if at any time in the future, anyone wants to talk with me about anything, you don't need an appointment. I'll be glad to see you."

This was no trumped up, contrived speech to gain the confidence of the Fidelity "family." His invitation to see him at any time, for any reason, without appointment turned out to be as bona-fide over the years as it was his first day in office as president.

Bob Roberts soon proved he had plenty of other assets—but the two chief assets he brought to the Fidelity will always be his *complete humility* and his *boundless enthusiasm.*

The Fidelity Mutual was founded in 1878. The year Bob Roberts became president, the company had $392,000,000 of insurance in force. Thirteen years later, the amount of insurance in force was increased by 300%! . . . a total volume of business three times greater in thirteen years . . . than it had achieved the entire first sixty-seven years they were in business!

Dale Carnegie, during his lifetime, interviewed some of the most famous people on earth; and Dale told me he found, in general, the greater they are, the easier they are to talk to, the more humble and human they are.

. . . When Benjamin Franklin drew up his original list of principles to help him become a better businessman, it contained only twelve. But when a friend convinced him that he was "generally thought to be proud"; that his pride showed itself frequently in conversation and manner; that many people disliked him for this, Ben determined to cure himself of this "vice or folly." So he added *Humility* to his list, "giving an extensive meaning to the word."

Adding "Humility" to his *"line-up,"* proved to be an important turning point in Ben's life! (And this, I think, is a tremendous thought): . . . Here, he had been exercising himself each week, trying to acquire the habit of those twelve other principles . . . yet he was losing friends and business!

By adopting just this *one more principle*, he began to win friends, and forge ahead in business!

By the time he was forty-two years old, Franklin, "Poor Richard," the name he used in much of his writing, was in a position to retire from his printing business and concentrate most of his time and energy on promoting an amazing number of worthy projects in the fields of science and invention; as well as countless other services for the good of mankind.

It is just possible that the Constitution of the United States might never have been adopted if it hadn't been for *Humility*. It was 1787. Franklin was eighty-one years old, and one of the chief framers. It began to look as though the Constitution Convention could never come to an agreement. Listen to Franklin's *humble* logic as he sold the delegation. At times, he appeared to be on the other side!

"I confess that I do not entirely approve of this Constitution at present; but, sir, I am not sure I shall *never* approve it; for having lived long, I have experienced many instances of being obliged, by better information or fuller consideration, to change opinions even on important subjects which I once thought right, but found to be otherwise.

"The older I grow, the more apt I am to doubt my own judgment of others. Most men, indeed, as well as most sects in religions, think themselves in possession of all truth. In these sentiments, sir, I agree to this Constitution, with all its faults— if they are such; because I think a general government necessary for us, and there is no form of government but what may be a blessing to the people, if well administered.

"On the whole, sir, I cannot help expressing a wish that every member of the convention who may still have objections to it would with me on this occasion doubt a little of his own infalli-bility, and to make manifest our unanimity *put his name to this instrument.*"

—AND THEY ALL SIGNED!

Years ago, I was inspired by a speech made by one of Amer-ica's greatest jurists—Judge Learned Hand. Standing bare-headed in the sun, before a group of newly naturalized citizens in New York's Central Park, he asked this question:

"What is the Spirit of Liberty? The spirit of liberty is the spirit which is not too sure that it is right; the spirit of liberty is the spirit which seeks to understand the minds of other men and women; the spirit of liberty is the spirit which weighs their interests alongside its own without bias; the spirit of liberty remembers that not even a sparrow falls to earth un-heeded; the spirit of liberty is the spirit of Him who, nearly 2,000 years ago, taught mankind that lesson it has never learned, but has never quite forgotten; that there may be a Kingdom where the least shall be heard and considered side by side with the greatest."

Adding *Humility* to his "line-up," proved to be an important turning point in Franklin's life! (This I think is a *tremendous* thought): Ben had been exercising himself each week, trying to acquire the habit of those twelve other Principles ... yet, he was losing friends and business!

> "He that falls in love with himself will have no rivals"
> *Poor Richard*

Chapter 32

THE COCKTAIL PARTY PRAYER MEETING

Out on the Nevada desert one glorious moonlight night, just below the great Hoover Dam, on Lake Meade, I saw a strange phenomenon. I was stretched out on the flat of my back, looking up at a million stars. Guests of the Lake Meade Lodge had built a huge bonfire on the beach from driftwood . . . then I saw it! The smoke from that roaring fire was spiraling up into the sky from right to left, like the hands of a clock *turning backward!*

I had heard of this strange power caused by the rotation of the Earth; and I wondered why this same power causes smoke south of the Equator to *reverse* the action and spiral in the direction followed by the hands of a clock.

And it can never be different!

Likewise, the winds in a cyclone *north* of the Equator spiral counter clockwise; *south* of the Equator they spiral clockwise.

Lying there on the beach, gazing up at the stars and a beautiful full moon, I began wondering about the miracle of the Earth making a complete revolution—24,000 miles every 24 hours—right to the split second! "In addition to that," I got to thinking, "here we are, on the beach by this quiet lake, in perfect peace, yet this same power is carrying the Earth like a great space ship, on a complete round trip, circling the Sun every 365 days ... the fantastic distance of *five hundred eighty-seven million miles every year!*"

Later that night in my room, I got out a pencil and figured it up on paper: we are traveling 18 miles a second around the Sun—a speed that would carry a plane across the Atlantic Ocean from New York to Paris—in three minutes!

Or, if you decided not to stop at Paris, you could keep on going, and be back in New York City in less than twenty-four minutes after you left—and rejoin your wife before she finished her breakfast!

... Not long afterward, I boarded a plane in Des Moines, Iowa, at seven o'clock in the morning. I was scheduled to speak that night in Toledo, Ohio. Shortly after we took off, a terrible wind and thunderstorm began tossing our two-motored plane around in the air. When we arrived over Chicago, a thick fog had blown in from the Great Lakes, bringing almost zero visibility. No incoming planes were permitted to land. After circling around more than an hour, the pilot announced that he had been instructed to go up to Milwaukee. When we reached Milwaukee, the fog was too heavy to make a landing there, so we were ordered to go on through to Toledo. But there, it was even worse, so we tried Cleveland. Same result. Great bolts of lightning flashed all around us. Violent thunderbolts shook the heavens. Our plane kept going, but no one seemed to know where.

Six o'clock that night, our pilot radioed the airport that our gas was running dangerously low. We were given the signal to descend. Everyone held his breath! Suddenly, we began bouncing on the ground, and the next thing we knew we came to a stop directly in front of the main building of the Cleveland Airport! Then, something happened in that plane I never saw happen before—nor since. Simultaneously, every one of us, twenty-four passengers, applauded! It was an applause quite different from any I ever heard before . . . I think we were all praying—not saying—*"Thank You God!"*—and *"Thank You!"* to the pilot.

I managed to get a sandwich and hot coffee at the lunch-counter. A westbound plane came in—the fog was lifting a bit, so they put me on. I arrived in Toledo just in time for the meeting. Three men were waiting at the airport to greet me. They had been there for hours.

As we drove out to the Scott High School Auditorium, where I was to make my talk, they told me the following extraordinary story:

"Gil" Dittmer, prominent insurance executive and chairman of this meeting, was giving a five-o'clock cocktail party at his home in my honor. Naturally, I was supposed to be there. Twelve committee members were enjoying a jolly party, because the meeting was a sell-out, and these men had all worked hard for it. But, as time went on, they began receiving frightening reports from the three members waiting at the airport. "One plane over Indiana crashed!" they said, "and Frank Bettger's plane is in trouble!" Later, when rumors started that the plane I was on was reported missing, the cocktail party developed into a *Prayer Meeting!*

"Some of those prayers," they told me later, "were the most fantastic God ever listened to, but we were all convinced that God heard us all right, because He never listened to more sincere, earnest praying!" One man declared, "A few of those prayers were delivered by men who hadn't prayed in years!"

I'm not recommending "cocktail party-prayer meetings" . . .

but I must admit, I'll always feel highly honored by the one
that was "rounded up" for me!

... Now, let me tell you about some of the thoughts I had
up there in that plane. I had plenty of time to think. Eleven
hours of it! During the worst part of the flight, I had a little
prayer-meeting all of my own! I seemed to be listening for the
most part. I heard nothing. Yet, a message seemed to come
to me just as clearly as if I did hear it! It was in the form of
questions ... like this:

... "Remember that night in Nevada on the beach at Lake
Meade, how you noticed the phenomenon of the smoke spiraling into the sky from right to left? ... And how it dawned on
you that the great Power controlling the movement of that
smoke is the same Power which controls and navigates the Sun,
the Stars, the Earth, and all the other planets? ...

"That God created this power, and the Laws; and is directing
all things on this earth. *He* has the only *Master Plan*. And *these*
laws—man can never revoke ... Remember? ...

"Do you know there is another great Law—created by this
same Power—controlling the destiny of man—the *Law of Right
and Wrong*?—and that this is another law man can never
revoke? ...

"Unknowingly—when you hit the sawdust trail and grasped
Billy Sunday's hand, you were making a decision to harness
your life to this *Great Power* ... Since that day, some miracu-
lous things have happened to the broken down ballplayer that
little mongrel brought away from the bridge in Chattanooga,
Tennessee. . . ."

These were some of the thoughts that kept running through
my head up there while we were being tossed around ten thousand feet in the air. Was I scared? Was I worried? Believe it
or not—No! I had a strange feeling of security. I had a *job*

to do. *This job.* And I believed I would be allowed to finish it. I believed this. I really did. I just *knew* I was going to get down out of that plane alive!

When I applauded *"Thank You!"* with all the other passengers, I wasn't applauding because fear had passed, and I was alive and breathing. I was saying *"Thank You!"* because I discovered my faith had been so real. I had experienced the Great Universal *Power of Faith!*

Fear is lack of Faith; lack of Faith is ignorance.

Faith is belief in the Power of Truth; the same irrevocable power which controls the movement of the Planets; the Universe.

Welcome Truth as you would welcome Sunlight. Love God and you will love Truth . . . for God *is* Truth—and God is Love.

> Here will I hold. If there's a Power above us (and that there is, all nature cries aloud thro' all her works), He must delight in Virtue; and that which He delights in must be happy.
>
> —Cato

Chapter 33

AN AMAZING INTERNATIONAL EVENT

THE YEAR 1956, witnessed an amazing International event. Nothing just like it had ever happened before in the history of civilization! More than 500,000,000 people—five hundred million!—of every race, color, and religious faith—in seventy-two countries throughout the world—celebrated the 250th anniversary of the birth of one of the wisest and most practical men who ever walked the face of the earth . . . Benjamin Franklin, the hero of this book!

The fact that this world-wide celebration continued throughout the entire year—not just for the anniversary of his birth, January 17th—made it highly significant.

Many of these nations issued special postage stamps with Franklin's picture on them, to honor him. Russia, for example, issued the very first stamp ever used by the Soviet Union to pay tribute to an American!

Why? What made this man so great?

What secret power did he possess? Did he inherit some kind of genius? . . .

Let's look at the records: Born in Boston, Massachusetts, in 1706, he was the fifteenth child in a family of ten sons and seven daughters. His father was a "poor, but respectable candle-maker." Not one of his seventeen children ever showed any unusual ability—except Ben!

What made this man great? Near the end of his long and amazing life, he revealed the secret . . . but first, let's look back a little.

When Ben first arrived in Philadelphia, he was only seventeen. Landing at the little wooden wharf at the foot of Market Street, he walked up the street with nothing but a loaf of bread under his arm, and a few pennies in his pocket. His whole appearance was somewhat bedraggled, because he had helped row a big open boat all the previous night, in a driving rainstorm down the Delaware River from Burlington, New Jersey, a distance of twenty-five miles.

Still munching on a piece of bread, between Third and Fourth Streets, he passed the home of Read, the carpenter, whose wife took in boarders, and "sold ointment for the cure of the itch!" Read's pretty daughter, Deborah, was standing at the door. She laughed at Ben, and thought he made a "most awkward, ridiculous appearance."

If someone had said to her: "Deborah, some day you are going to marry that young man and he is going to become one of the most famous men on the face of this earth," Deborah probably would have replied: "You are positively crazy. He looks like he doesn't even have enough sense to come in out of the rain!"

And—if someone had told the young man how famous he was going to become, he probably would have answered: "Look, mister, all I want to do is make a decent living. I've had only two years of schooling, but I worked in a printing shop in Boston. Do you know where there's a printer in town? I'd like to go there and see if I can get a job!"

. . . But this was a Sunday morning, so Ben went to church, Christ Church, on Second Street, above Market.

That was two hundred and thirty-seven years ago. Yet, that church remains on the same spot today. It is a very beautiful church, still holding regular services. My wife and I attend services there often with our daughter, Lee. When you come to Philadelphia—regardless of your faith—why not make it a point to visit this historic landmark? It is open daily to the public from 9:00 A.M. to 5:00 P.M. No one is a stranger in Christ Church.

Wouldn't you like to sit in the same pew where Benjamin Franklin sat and worshipped? You may. I have sat in that pew many times. It does something for me. I'm sure it will do something for you. . . .

There is a story told about that first time young Ben went into old Christ Church. After he had been sitting there for quite a spell, with nothing happening, he leaned forward to the man sitting in front of him and whispered: "Sir, when does the service begin?" The man whispered back: "Immediately after we leave here!"

. . . Then Ben fell sound asleep! But don't forget—he had been rowing a boat all night!

Whether or not that story is true, what that man is said to have whispered to him that Sunday morning, turned out to be the biggest thing in Benjamin Franklin's life . . . *Service!*
Performance!

He came to believe that words, without *performance,* were of little value. Years later, he wrote: "God ought to be worshipped by adoration, prayer, and thanksgiving . . . *but that the most acceptable service of God is doing good to man."*
THAT'S WHEN THE SERVICE BEGINS!

So—included in his *list of thirteen principles,* was *Resolution*: "Resolution, once it became habitual," he wrote, "would keep me firm in my endeavors to obtain all the subsequent principles."

Here are just a few of his performances of "service in doing good to man": diplomat; scientist; physicist; printer; author; publisher; philosopher; inventor—with 105 inventions to his credit; First Postmaster General of the U. S. Postal System—which he organized; Founder of many great institutions, such as The University of Pennsylvania; The Pennsylvania Hospital —the first hospital in America; The Philadelphia Library—the first free library in America; The First Fire Insurance Company; etc. etc.

And when his life of service had ended, he left legacies to the cities of Boston and Philadelphia, which now total over two million dollars, to help young married men who have served an apprenticeship as skilled workers, mechanics, and other trades, start in business for themselves! . . . As recently as January, 1960, the Massachusetts Supreme Court refused to terminate the trust fund established by Benjamin Franklin in 1790. The court said it saw no good reason to interfere with Franklin's original plan to continue the fund until 1991, the date set in his Will.

How could any one "ordinary man" acquire such "extraordinary ability?" Near the end of his long and amazing life, in his own handwriting, Benjamin Franklin revealed the source of his great power—a scientific device so simple that even a twelve year old child can understand and use it!

Here it is—abridged:

> . . . It may be well my posterity should be informed that to this *little artifice* (the list of thirteen principles) their ancestor owed his long-continued health and good

constitution; the acquisition of his fortune; the confidence of his country; the honors conferred upon him; and *all his success and happiness* ... to the joint influence of the *whole mass of the thirteen principles*, even in the imperfect state he was able to acquire them, which make his company still sought for, and agreeable even to his younger acquaintances. *I hope, therefore, that some of my descendants may follow the example, and reap the benefit.*

... Now, why did five hundred million people in every corner of this planet pay homage in 1956 to this wise and humble man? Was it because of his great genius, or his many great accomplishments which I have just mentioned? No! Not because of *any* of them!

These nations and peoples dedicated an entire year to honor and study the life of Benjamin Franklin because Franklin, though an American, was in truth the *"First Citizen of the World"* whose ideals belong to every individual, regardless of race, color, religion or nationality. They were honoring the man who believed "the supreme objective of civilization is to establish an enduring peace" ... and who laid down a "Three-Step-Plan for World Peace," which the world has just begun to recognize.

Strangely enough, Franklin estimated that "the goal might be accomplished in 150 to 200 years." That would bring it to pass before 1980! And when this supreme event comes to pass, we are going to witness the greatest period of prosperity and happiness in the history of mankind. Untold benefits will accrue to all the peoples of the world. Just a fraction of the billions now spent for wars and preparation for wars will be employed in public works; the extension of agriculture—enough to feed more than twice the present population of the earth; millions of lives will be saved annually through the wider spread of medical knowledge, lengthen the life span in every country; and bring to every land an abundance of conveniences and comforts of living, through the accomplishments of science;— devoted to the needs of man, instead of destroying the lives of so many thousands of working people who might have performed the useful labor.

When can World Peace begin? Right now! We haven't got much more time. Franklin estimated the deadline at 1980. To meet that deadline, we must start now! Later, may be too late!

... How will World Peace begin? The solution hinges on three psychological laws:

1. PREPARATION ... Plans and specifications will be drafted by the world's most able architects, engineers, scientists, doctors, agriculturists, industrialists, etc. etc. for the greatest event in human history—the conquest of poverty and the elimination of famine everywhere.

2. ACTION—Enthusiastic ACTION ... Able administrators, entrusted with the direction and execution of these plans in a series of five or ten year Timing Schedules.

3. UNIVERSAL DISARMAMENT ... This will begin simultaneously with Steps 1 and 2. All mankind will be astounded as the momentum builds up, producing a new form of civilization:

> *that man everywhere may be free to walk the earth with dignity; peacefully to fulfill the greatness in his soul; to worship God in reverence and good works; to end cruelty toward one another....*
> —B. FRANKLIN

... For it is not by the sword that God will deliver us from the curse of hate and fear, but with the universal Brotherhood of Love.

... Mr. Franklin, Sir, in this 254th year since your birth, we pause to voice humble thanks for the priceless legacy you have bequeathed to all men; and for your ideas and ideals that may soon help us become a United Nations of individuals under one flag, drawn together under God by a true and enduring spirit of Brotherly Love.

... Mr. Franklin, Sir, we thank you.

Chapter 34

A LETTER FROM ME TO YOU

W HEN I FIRST THOUGHT of producing this book, I was frightened by the magnitude of the job, and fully aware of my limitations for such an undertaking. Then I recalled almost the last thing Franklin ever wrote:

> I have always thought that one man, of tolerable abilities, may work great changes, and accomplish great affairs among mankind, if he makes the execution of this plan his sole study and business ... but he should have *first* exercised himself with the thirteen weeks' examination and practiced the principles long enough to reap the benefit. . . .

This seemed like a challenge to me. I reasoned it this way: "You were given the prescription by Doctor Franklin. You had the prescription filled. You *took* it! *And you have reaped the benefit!*"

It has become like a TORCH I got hold of. And, through this book, I hope to make it burn bright enough for someone else to take hold of—someone far more able than I to hand it on to future generations.

I thought the best way for me to explain this great legacy of Franklin's—instead of trying to preach or lecture—was to tell you a story. The story of what it did for me, and what it will do for *anyone* who will apply it. Here it is. I hope you like it.

Enthusiastically *Yours!*

FRANK BETTGER

THE 13 PRINCIPLES

1. *Enthusiasm*

Make a high and holy resolve that you will double the amount of enthusiasm that you have been putting into your work and into your life! . . . If you carry out that resolve, and apply this ingredient to every one of the thirteen principles during the next thirteen weeks, be prepared to see astonishing results. It will probably double your income, and double your happiness.

"If you can give your son or daughter only one
gift, let it be Enthusiasm!"

. . . Bruce Barton

2. *Order: Self-Organization*

If you want to know whether you're going to be a success in your business, or whatever your calling in life may be, the test is easy: *Can you organize and control your time?* If not, drop out, for you will surely fail! You may not think so, but you will fail as surely as you live . . .

If you want to enjoy one of the greatest luxuries in life—the

---

* My Line-up as first applied just to selling appears in my books on selling. *How I Raised Myself from Failure to Success in Selling*, and *How I Multiplied My Income and Happiness in Selling*, published by Prentice-Hall, Inc., Englewood Cliffs, N. J. Special cards based on this line-up have been distributed throughout the world, by Dartnell Corporation, Chicago, Illinois.

luxury of having enough time—time to play; time to rest; time
to *think things through*; time to get things done and know you
have done them to the best of your ability; remember there is
only *one* way: Take enough *time* to think and plan things in
the order of their importance. Your life will take on a new zest.
You will add years to your life—and more *life* to your years!

Let all your things have their places; let each part of your
business have its time.   FRANKLIN

3. *Others*

Remember what Christy Mathewson said: "Throwing a ball
without a target is like shooting a gun off into the air. *No gunner ever became a sharpshooter without aiming at the Bull's-
Eye!*"

Applied to everyday living: *Find out what the other person
wants, then help him find the best way to get it* ... The ancients
first said it. It's *The Golden Rule* in *action!*

> "... accept my kind offices to Thy other children
> as the only return in my power for Thy continual
> favors to me."

> (*Closing words of Franklin's daily prayer*)

4. *Questions*

Imitate Socrates. Questions, rather than positive assertions
are the most effective way to find out what people want or
need ... *Inquire* rather than *attack*.

Show that you respect the other person's point of view.

> "*When truth and error have fair play, the former
> is always an overmatch for the latter*" ...FRANKLIN

One of the biggest things you get out of a college education
is a questioning attitude, a habit of demanding and weighing
evidence ... a scientific approach.

If you have a decision to make of great importance—try the Algebraic Method:

Why?	Why Not?

5. *Silence: Listen*

Show the other person that you are sincerely interested in what he is saying; give him all the eager attention and appreciation that he craves and is so hungry for, but seldom gets. *Listen with enthusiasm!* If you would be a good conversationalist, remember: "The wit of conversation consists more in finding it in Others, than showing a great deal to yourself."

A MAGIC *three-point formula*:

1. Find out what the other person is interested in.
2. Try to direct his conversation with questions he will enjoy answering.
3. Then, *LISTEN!*

PRAYER

For This Week

"O God, lift me out of the rush and the turmoil of life, that I may find the strength that comes from fellowshhip with Thee. Give me a quiet mind, a teachable heart and a willingness to wait on Thy guidance and direction. May I learn how to listen as well as to speak, and in the stillness may I hear Thy voice. Refresh me in the quiet hour for the responsibilities of the day ... through Jesus Christ.

Amen."

—Alfred Grant Walton, Brooklyn, N. Y.

Minister, Flatbush-Tompkins Congregational Church

6. *Resolution*

"Resolve to perform what you ought; perform without fail what you resolve. Resolution, once it becomes habitual will keep you firm in your endeavors to obtain all the subsequent Principles"   FRANKLIN

In this world, we either discipline ourselves, or we are disciplined by the world. I prefer to discipline myself. Franklin said: "Disobedience is slavery; obedience is *liberty.*"

... "Gabby" Street said: "Lick him in the first round!"

... The Scriptures say: *He that conquers himself is greater than he that taketh the city.*

7. *Frugality*

"If you would be *free,* think of saving as well as *getting*; away then with your expensive follies, and you will not then have much cause to complain of hard times and heavy taxes. As Poor Richard says, 'The second Vice is lying, the first is running into debt. And lying rides upon debt's back.' Preserve your freedom; maintain your independence; be frugal and free ... this doctrine, my friends is reason and wisdom. Profit by this wisdom."

Pay Yourself First!

8. *Sincerity*

"Use no hurtful deceit; think innocently and justly, and if you speak, speak accordingly."   FRANKLIN

To win and hold the confidence of others, Rule One is: *Deserve Confidence*—Have the strength of character to be true when no one else will know the difference. Not—will the other person believe it. The *real* test is do *you* believe it?

9. *Praise vs. Criticism*

The best way to destroy an enemy:—Apply the Principle of one of the world's greatest diplomats, Benjamin Franklin: *I will speak ill of no man—and speak all the good I know of everybody.*

Everybody likes to feel important. People are hungry for praise—not flattery—but honest, sincere appreciation. . . during my years in baseball, I never saw criticism do anything but harm to ballplayers. But I saw honest *praise* and *encouragement* make stars out of ordinary players. After retiring from baseball I saw these principles produce the same results in *business* and in the *home!*

10. *Health*

Food:

Chew each mouthful 32 times. You'll double one of the greatest pleasures in life; you'll be free from indigestion; you will maintain your normal weight and live longer!

Exercise:

Try to get some form of exercise daily. (But avoid excess or violent activities after forty.) One of the most beneficial forms of exercise is a good, luxurious S-T-R-E-T-C-H before getting out of bed in the morning; a "seventh inning" stretch a couple of times each day only takes a few moments. Improves your posture, keeps you supple and fit!

Rest Frequently:

If possible, take a twenty minute nap before evening dinner or after lunch. Relax often. Loosen collar, shoes and belt when taking a nap or sitting for a long while.

Change shoes for slippers when home; many men are now doing this in the office.

Health Examination:

We have compulsory car inspection laws for safety and longer life of the car. Why not apply the same common sense to the *human* machine? Have a complete medical check-up once a year; dentist check-up every six-months; likewise eyes tested every couple of years.

11. *Happiness*

The most common prayer: "Lord, help me!"

The most uncommon prayer: "Thank you, Father."

Be not disturbed at trifles, or accidents common
    or unavoidable.   FRANKLIN

Give every living soul you meet the *best* SMILE—
    you ever SMILED in your life. It is one of the best
    ways to stop worrying, and start living!

Great beauty, great strength, and great riches, are
    really and truly of no great use. A right heart ex-
    ceeds all.   FRANKLIN

12. *Humility*

... Adding *Humility* to his *"line-up"*, proved to be an important turning point in Franklin's life! (This I think is a *tremendous* thought): Ben had been exercising himself each week, trying to acquire the habit of those twelve other Principles ... yet, he was losing friends and business! ...

"He that falls in love with himself will have no rivals."

POOR RICHARD

13. *Faith*

Fear is lack of Faith; lack of Faith is ignorance. Faith is

belief in the Power of Truth; the same irrevocable power which controls the movement of the Planets; the Universe.

Welcome Truth as you would welcome Sunlight. Love God and you will love Truth . . . for God *is* Truth—and God is Love.

Here will I hold. If there's a Power above us (and that there is, all nature cries aloud thro' all her works), He must delight in Virtue; and that which He delights in must be happy.   Cato

INDEX

G

General Electric Company, 105
Giants, 20
God, 38, 108, 111, 135, 169, 180,
    181, 183, 186, 189, 194
Golden Rule, The, 94
Gotch, Frank, 163
Groskin, Horace, 45, 46, 51, 53

H

Hamilton, Billy, 152-153, 154, 155
Hand, Learned, 176
Happiness, 194
Harris and Taylor, 132
Harvard University, 69, 168
Health, 158-165, 194
    breathing, 162
    check-ups, 165
    chewing, 160-161
    death rate, 158, 161
    diseases, 158-159, 162, 164
    exercise, 159, 163-164, 165
    Fletcherizing, 160-161
    food, 160-161, 165
    life expectancy, 158-159
    rest, 164, 165
    stretching, 163-164, 165
    weight, 161, 164
Heart diseases, 162, 164
Hebrew Laws, 164
Heintz, Leo I., 49
Hershey, Milton, 98-100
Highlanders, 13
Hodge, Charles G., 39
*How I Multiplied My Income and
    Happiness in Selling*, 192n
*How I Raised Myself from Failure
    to Success in Selling*, 192n
Huggins, Miller, 21, 22, 24, 30, 31,
    36, 41, 49, 58, 59, 60-61,
    62-63, 65, 73-74, 80, 83,
    155-156
Humility, 172, 174-175, 177, 194
Hunsicker, Clayton M., 53, 70, 88,
    89, 90, 128, 130, 142-143

I

Ignorance, 183

Independence, 193
Indigestion, 165
Inquirer, humble, 96
Inquiries, 104, 193
International League, 31
Isaiah, 194

J

James, William, 168
Jesus, 108, 164, 176
Johnson, Walter, 125
*Journal of the Heart Association of
    Pennsylvania*, 162
Justice, 193

K

Keith's Theatre, 159
Kennedy, Sam, 18, 118
Knotts, Joe, 6
Konetchy, Mr., 155
Kooperman, Mr., 114

L

Lake Meade, 178, 181
Landis, Kenesaw Mountain, 144-,
    145
Landy, John, 76
Lapp, Jack, 117, 118
Leach, Tommy, 154-155
"Leadership Training, Human Re-
    lations and Salesmanship," iii
Lee, Ivy, 67-68
Liberty, spirit of, 176
Lie detector, 141-142
Life expectancy, 158
Line-up, 57-59, 192-194
Listener, 24
Listening, 105-109, 181, 193
Litchenstein, Mr., 31
Louis, Joe, 137
Love, 190
    Brotherhood of, 189
Ludlow, Ben, 167, 168
Lying, 140

M

McCarthy, "Bowels," 49

Recommended Readings

- Siddhartha by Hermann Hesse, www.bnpublishing.net

- The Anatomy of Success, Nicolas Darvas, www.bnpublishing.net

- The Dale Carnegie Course on Effective Speaking, Personality Development, and the Art of How to Win Friends & Influence People, Dale Carnegie, www.bnpublishing.net

- The Law of Success In Sixteen Lessons by Napoleon Hill (Complete, Unabridged), Napoleon Hill, www.bnpublishing.net

- It Works, R. H. Jarrett, www.bnpublishing.net

- The Art of Public Speaking (Audio CD), Dale Carnegie, wwww.bnpublishing.net

- The Success System That Never Fails (Audio CD), W. Clement Stone, www.bnpublishing.net

CPSIA information can be obtained at www.ICGtesting.com
Printed in the USA
LVOW011631220213

321348LV00018B/1008/P

9 781607 963943